A Manual of the Excellent Man

Uttamapurisa Dīpanī

A Manual of the Excellent Man

Uttamapurisa Dīpanī

The Venerable Ledi Sayādaw

Translated into Burmese by

U Tin Oo (Myaung)

Edited by

Bhikkhu Pesala

BPE

BPS Pariyatti Editions

BPS Pariyatti Editions
An imprint of Pariyatti Publishing
www.pariyatti.org

Published by Buddhist Publication Society, Kandy, Sri Lanka, 1977, 1985, 1998.

Published with the consent of the original publisher.

First BPS Pariyatti Edition, 2016
ISBN: 978-1-938754-94-4 (Print)
ISBN: 978-1-938754-93-7 (PDF eBook)
ISBN: 978-1-938754-91-3 (ePub)
ISBN: 978-1-938754-92-0 (Mobi)
Library of Congress Control Number: 2016911952

Printed in the USA

Contents

Publisher's Foreword to the American Edition

In recent years, many people in the West have been exposed to the teachings of the Buddha through the practice of Vipassana meditation as taught by S.N. Goenka. Mr. Goenka was born in Burma (now Myanmar) where he learned this technique of meditation from Sayagyi U Ba Khin, who had in turn been taught by Saya Thetgyi. Saya Thetgyi had the fortune to learn Vipassana from the highly respected scholar and meditator monk Ledi Sayadaw.

In Burma, Ledi Sayadaw is well known, and in his lifetime was the author of more than 100 books that provided both clarification and inspiration regarding the teachings of the Buddha. As Vipassana meditation in the tradition of Ledi Sayadaw begins to spread in the West, we are fortunate to begin to gain broader access to his writings as well.

We are grateful to the Buddhist Publication Society of Sri Lanka for allowing us to co-publish *The Manual of an Excellent Man*. It is our sincere wish that this publication will prove valuable to those interested in understanding the Buddha's teaching at a deeper level, while providing the inspiration to continue walking step by step on the path.

Editor's Foreword

For Burmese Buddhists, Venerable Ledi Sayādaw needs no introduction, since his fame is legendary. Many Buddhists outside Burma will also have read his Manuals of Buddhism, or at least extracts from it such as the *Maggaṅga Dīpanī* or the *Bodhipakkhiya Dīpanī*, which are both published by the Buddhist Publication Society. As the name implies, a Dīpanī is a work that illuminates the subject, so we can call it a "manual" or an "exposition." The Venerable Ledi Sayādaw is deservedly famous for his expositions, of which he wrote more than seventy. All of them show his deep learning of the Pāḷi texts and commentaries, but this work especially urges Buddhists not to be content with mere devotion or academic learning, but to take up insight meditation in earnest to gain penetrative knowledge of the Noble Truths.

The Venerable Ledi Sayādaw was the "father" of the insight meditation tradition in Burma. Before he became famous, only a few monks practised insight meditation, and even fewer lay people. He lived during the time of the British Raj, when many ignorant Buddhists were converting to Christianity. At the same time, English scholars were studying Buddhism. The Venerable Ledi Sayādaw replied to some questions in Pāḷi put by Mrs Caroline Rhys Davids, who was then working on the translation of the Pāḷi texts into English.

The origin of this edition deserves some mention since it has been so long in coming to print. I think it was in 1991 that James Patrick Stewart-Ross, an American Buddhist, visited me at the Burmese Vihāra in Wembley, England and gave me a stack of computer disks, on which were more than thirty voluminous works by various authors. Many of them were by the Venerable Ledi Sayādaw. Mr Ross had spent many years collecting works by famous Burmese Sayādaws and had made heroic efforts to get English translations made. While living in Thailand, he made many trips into Burma, to search out able translators and typists to help him with this colossal undertaking.

During the following years, I gradually sifted through the works I had been given and picked out a few that seemed most worthy of publication. Among the best were the *Uttamapurisa Dīpanī* and the *Dāna Dīpanī*, both by the Venerable Ledi Sayādaw. I edited these two works and printed out a few copies, but I lost touch with Mr Ross. It was not until 1997 that I met him again in Burma. Meanwhile I had had some correspondence with Bhikkhu Bodhi of the Buddhist Publication Society, and he agreed that the *Uttamapurisa Dīpanī* was worth publishing. While in Burma, I worked through the entire book several times, removing many Pāḷi passages that I thought would be too intimidating for most modern readers, and I improved the grammar to the best of my ability. I hope the result will be acceptable. Reconciling the need for simplicity with that for authenticity is difficult, but I have tried to retain the spirit of the author's work. At the same time I hope it will now be easier for the non-Buddhist or new Buddhist to appreciate the Sayādaw's inspiring teaching, which it should be noted, was addressed specifically to a devout and learned lay Buddhist.

Those who are familiar with the Pāḷi Canon will have no difficulty in following the thread of the Sayādaw's arguments, since the sources from which he quotes are quite well known. I have therefore not tried to provide a thorough list of references as I might have done for a more scholarly work. The Sayādaw's central theme is that no amount of academic learning will save one from rebirth in the lower realms, or in hell, if the pernicious wrong view of a belief in a permanent self, soul, or ego is not uprooted by the practice of insight meditation.

Several people objected to the frequent references to hell, some said it had "Christian connotations," even my computer's grammar checker said it was "offensive." However, I have resolutely retained it in most places. I think there is little difference between Buddhism and Christianity (or other religions) on this point. Most religions warn of dire consequences for those who do immoral deeds due to their lack of religious faith. If the readers are apprehensive even at the mention of the word, let them take up the practice of insight meditation to find sure release from the suffering of hell. Let them practise the real Dhamma of the Buddha by trying to comprehend the arising and vanishing of phenomena within their own body and mind. The Buddhist scriptures wholeheartedly endorse the Sayādaw's opinions, so if you have any doubts, please refer to the Nakhasikhā Sutta, which he quotes.

The 1969 Burmese second edition, which I referred to occasionally, was full of quotations from the Pāḷi texts, commentaries and subcommentaries. Most of these have been removed, leaving only the English translation, to make the book more readable for those who are not scholars. Quotation marks are used, even where the source is not given, to indicate that they are not the Sayādaw's own words. Aphorisms coined by the Sayādaw are indicated by a bolder typeface.

In the initial draft, there was some inconsistency in the dates. Working back from B.E. 1359 (1998) 1261 should have been 1900, not 1899 as stated, and the completion date (of 1262) was given as 1901. So I asked a friend to consult a 100-year calendar. It turned out that the Sayādaw received Maung Thaw's letter on 9th March, 1900 and completed the work on 28th April, the same year! (The Burmese New Year begins in April). The Sayādaw had indeed been burning the midnight oil for an early reply. I have been working on this edition (among many other works, it must be said) for at least eight years, but the Sayādaw completed it in just seven weeks.

Preface to the First Edition

More than two thousand years have passed since the Buddha, the Sākyan prince who showed the path to nibbāna, the founder of the Saṅgha, the most exalted and incomparable one, attained parinibbāna. The Burmese capital of Mandalay has fallen, its king dethroned, and the sun has set on Burma. The country is now ruled (by the British) from London in England, a European land. Now, there is in Mandalay an association founded by a group of modern educated Burmese. They are conversant in foreign languages and devoted to the discussion, preservation, and propagation of the Buddha's teaching.

The Honorary Secretary of the association is Maung Thaw, a clerk in the office of the Inspector of Schools. A tireless worker, Maung Thaw discussed religion with various non-Buddhist religious teachers and debated some knotty problems. He recorded several points raised on those occasions. He wanted an authoritative decision on the problems, so he approached the Venerable Mahāvisuddhārāma Sayādaw, an eminent leader of the Saṅgha in Mandalay.

This Venerable Sayādaw found the questions profound and subtle like the ones put by Sakka, Lord of the Tāvatiṃsa realm, to the Buddha. He remarked that such questions deserved to be tackled by Ledi Sayādaw of Monywa, who is not only learned, but has led an exemplary religious life. He accordingly sent a letter to the Venerable Ledi Sayādaw, with Maung Thaw's questions, for solution.

Although it was usual for Ledi Sayādaw to reply to religious questions immediately, on the present questions, received through the Venerable Mahāvisuddhārāma Sayādaw, he took time to answer them. He wanted to be thorough. He considered the questions in the light of various arguments, collated authorities on the points he wanted to make, and added his own illustrations.

He did not merely answer the questions. It was his intention to give a practical course on the development of insight. This alone can root out personality view, the ego, the so-called "self" that has possessed all sentient beings throughout saṃsāra. So, here we have an exposition on the Excellent Man (*uttamapurisa*) leading to enlightenment along the three stages of comprehension that penetrate the real nature of psychophysical phenomena.

THE VENERABLE LEDI SAYĀDAW'S REPLY

This is addressed to Maung Thaw.

Maung Thaw's petition, with the Venerable Mahāvisuddhārāma Sayādaw's endorsement, reached me on the tenth waxing day of Tabaung, 1261 Burmese Era (9th March, 1900 AD). It contains:

i. matters on doctrinal aspects that need to be explained;
ii. an expression of your desire to train for the development of insight;
iii. a request to show how one may advance from being a blind worldling to become a wise and virtuous person.

A blind worldling (*andhaputhujjana*) is one who has no "eye" of knowledge (of the Dhamma); a virtuous ordinary person (*kalyāṇaputhujjana*) is one who has the "eye" of knowledge.

There are four kinds of eyes of knowledge, namely:

1. the eye of right view;
2. the eye of learning or scriptural knowledge;
3. the eye of insight acquired through mental development, which is right view on the threshold of supramundane knowledge;
4. the eye of right view or supramundane knowledge.

Outside the Buddha's Era, when the teaching of the Buddha has fallen silent, a virtuous person who has developed concentration and has the first right view, can be called a virtuous ordinary person. However, during the times of the Buddha's teaching (*Buddhasāsana*), neither the first nor the second kind makes a virtuous ordinary person. One can be called a virtuous ordinary person only by gaining right view through insight, having understood the elements (*dhātu*) and the causative law (*paccaya*), thus dispelling personality view (*sakkāyadiṭṭhi*) and doubt (*vicikicchā*).

Such a person may develop supramundane knowledge, the fourth kind of eye, in this very life. Failing that, he or she may attain to that knowledge in the next life as a deva. If not, he or she may become a Solitary Buddha when the Buddha's teaching has fallen silent in the world. If one has the foundation for enlightenment, one will very easily realize the Dhamma under the teaching of a future Buddha as a human being or a deva. While the Buddha's teaching is extant (as at the present), only one who attains insight knowledge is called a virtuous ordinary person. Meritorious deeds such as almsgiving (*dāna*) and virtue (*sīla*) are not sufficient to deserve that status. Nor is any amount of scriptural learning. This is not a flattering description of a virtuous ordinary person; the scriptures say so.

Regarding your request for some cardinal principles in the Buddha's teaching to be borne in mind that can withstand any onslaught by heretics:

If it were only for discussion among our own compatriots, a reference to a good authority would suffice; practical illustrations may not be necessary. However, when it comes to the logician or the practical experimenter, espousing a different religion, scriptural authority will not suffice. With such people, cogent explanations supported by verifiable evidence are necessary to silence them. That being my main consideration, coupled with the Venerable Mahāvisuddhārāma Sayādaw's endorsement on your zeal in this field, I have based my answers to your queries on the Khandhavagga Saṃyutta. I have elaborated on it so that you can gain a clear grasp of the groundwork of Buddhism. To this end I have used plain Burmese. Profuse illustrations are given on abstruse topics for better comprehension.

Do not feel that it is thin on Pāḷi quotations. Too many quotations from the texts, I am afraid, will mar my arguments. With dependence on Pāḷi, it would be difficult to present a passable lecture, let alone silence the challenge of alien religions. There is not much point in formal lectures; what is important is to acquire the eye of insight-knowledge. The style is terse because the elucidation of my theme requires direct speech. Perhaps at certain places it might prove too terse for you. That is because I have been burning the midnight oil for an early reply to you.

So, I would ask you first to read it alone. Only if you have followed it, should you show it to others. If you have any stumbling blocks, refer them to the Venerable Mahāvisuddhārāma Sayādaw, and not to anyone else. When King Bimbisāra of Rājagaha sent a book on the Dhamma to King Pakkusāti of Taxila, he added a warning not to open it in front of others. If you have understood my answers, wish to preach to others and would like to add quotations, you can ask the Venerable Mahāvisuddhārāma Sayādaw, showing him where you wish to add them. Otherwise, you may write to me. If there are any points that are unclear to you, write to me without delay.

Ledi Sayādaw
2nd Waxing day of Kason, 1262 BE
29th April, 1900 CE

A Manual of the Excellent Man

Uttamapurisa Dīpanī

Namo Tassa Bhagavato Arahato Sammāsambuddhassa
Homage to the Exalted One, the Worthy One,
The Supremely Enlightened Buddha

Preamble

I shall answer concisely the nine questions posed by Maung Thaw, Office Clerk of the Inspector of Schools, Mandalay, according to the canonical texts and commentaries, giving my conclusions on doctrinal points.

Chapter One

The petition sent from Mandalay by Maung Thaw on the tenth waxing day of Tabaung, 1261 Burmese Era (9th March, 1900) contained nine questions. The first question was about the perfections:

5. Regarding the five aspirants: (i) a Perfectly Enlightened Buddha *(sammāsambuddha)*, (ii) a Solitary Buddha *(paccekabuddha)*, (iii) a Chief Disciple *(aggasāvaka)*, (iv) a Great Disciple *(mahāsāvaka)* and, (v) an Ordinary Disciple *(pakatisāvaka)*, how does the aspirant fulfil the perfections *(pāramī)* to achieve his respective goal?
6. May I know the definition, nature, and significance of the ten perfections, with particular reference to an aspirant to Supreme Enlightenment?

The Perfections Defined

In answer to the first question, regarding the definition, nature, and significance of the perfections, there are these ten perfections.

"Dānaṃ sīlañca nekkhammaṃ
Paññā viriya khantīca
Saccādhiṭṭhāna mettāca
Upekkhā pāramī dasa."

1) Giving *(dāna)*, 2) morality *(sīla)*, 3) renunciation *(nekkhamma)*, 4) wisdom *(paññā)*, 5) energy *(viriya)*, 6) patience *(khanti)*, 7) truthfulness *(sacca)*, 8) resolve *(adhiṭṭhāna)*, 9) loving-kindness *(mettā)*, 10) equanimity *(upekkhā)*.

The Nature of the Perfections

The nature of the perfections will be shown by their characteristic *(lakkhaṇa)*, function *(rasa)*, manifestation *(paccupaṭṭhāna)*, and proximate cause *(padaṭṭhāna)*. The ten perfections are mentioned in the Cariyapiṭaka Commentary and the Sīlakkhandha Subcommentary.

1. *Pariccāgalakkhaṇaṃ dānaṃ,*
   Deyyadhamma lobhaviddhaṃsanarasaṃ.
   Anāsatta paccupaṭṭhānaṃ,
   Pariccajitabba vatthu padaṭṭhānaṃ.

Dāna: It has the characteristic of generosity; its function is to destroy attachment to things by giving them away; it is manifested as non-attachment to things given away; its proximate cause is something in hand that would serve as a gift.

2. *Sīlanalakkhaṇaṃ sīlaṃ,*
   Dussīlya viddhaṃsanarasaṃ.
   Soceyya paccupaṭṭhānaṃ,
   Hirī-ottappa padaṭṭhānaṃ.

Sīla: It has the characteristic of keeping good bodily and verbal actions; its function is to destroy unwholesome or unruly bodily or verbal actions; it is manifested as purity of verbal actions; its proximate causes are moral shame *(hirī)* and moral dread *(ottappa)*.

3. *Kāmato bhavatoca, nikkhamanalakkhaṇaṃ nekkhammaṃ.*
Kāmabhavādīnavavibhāvanarasaṃ,
Tasseva vimukhabhāva paccupaṭṭhānaṃ,
Saṃvega padaṭṭhānaṃ.

Nekkhamma: Its characteristic is renouncing sensuality and thereby gaining release from becoming; its function is to purify and thus reveal the dangers of sensuality and of existence; it is manifested as avoidance of sensual desires; its proximate cause is a dread of sensuality through farsighted trepidation.

4. *Yathā sabhāva paṭivedhalakkhaṇā paññā,*
Visayobhāsanarasā.
Asammoha paccupaṭṭhānā,
Samādhi padaṭṭhānā.

Paññā: It has the characteristic of seeing things in their true nature; its function is to shed light on all objects of sense; it is manifested as non-confusion; its proximate cause is concentration.

5. *Ussāhalakkhaṇaṃ viriyaṃ,*
Upatthambhanarasaṃ.
Asaṃsīdana paccupaṭṭhānaṃ,
Saṃvega padaṭṭhānaṃ.

Viriya: It has the characteristic of diligence; its function is to brace one up; it is manifested as persistence; its proximate cause is a sense of urgency arising from farsighted trepidation of birth, decay, sickness, death, and all attendant ills.

6. *Khamanalakkhaṇā khanti,*
Iṭṭhāniṭṭha sahanarasā.
Adhivāsana paccupaṭṭhānā,
Yathābhūtadassana padaṭṭhānā.

Khanti: It has the characteristic of tolerance; its function is not to be moved by likes or dislikes; it is manifested as forbearance in the face of the gravest provocation; its proximate cause is seeing things as they really are.

7. *Avisaṃvādanalakkhaṇaṃ saccaṃ,*
   Yathāvavibhāvanarasaṃ.
   Sādhutā paccupaṭṭhānaṃ,
   Soracca padaṭṭhānaṃ.

Sacca: It has the characteristic of not misleading others by one's utterance; its function is to discover the truth as one sees or knows; it is manifested as sweet and agreeable speech; its proximate cause is a sympathetic tenderness towards all.

8. *Bodhisambhāresu avaṭṭhāna lakkhaṇaṃ adhiṭṭhānaṃ,*
   Tesaṃ paṭipakkhābhibhavana rasaṃ.
   Tattha acalatā paccupaṭṭhānaṃ,
   Bodhisambhāra padaṭṭhānaṃ.

Adhiṭṭhāna: It has the characteristic of resolve in undertaking meritorious deeds for fulfilling the perfections; its function is to overcome all opposition and obstacles that lie in one's path; it is manifested as firmness in one's stand; its proximate cause lies in those very meritorious deeds, such as generosity, when one is practising for perfections.

9. *Hitākārappavatti lakkhaṇā mettā,*
   Hitūpasaṃhāra rasā.
   Sommābhāva paccupaṭṭhānā,
   Sattānaṃ manāpabhāva dassana padaṭṭhānā.

Mettā: It has the characteristic of promoting the welfare of others; its function is being solicitous of others' welfare; it is manifested as a helpful attitude; its proximate cause is seeing only the good of others.

10. *Majjhattākārappavatti lakkhaṇā upekkhā,*
Samabhāvadassana rasā.
Paṭighānunaya vūpasama paccupaṭṭhānā,
Kammassakatā paccavekkhaṇā padaṭṭhānā.

Upekkhā: It has the characteristic of equanimity in the face of praise and blame; its function is to neutralize one's emotions; it is manifested as impartiality; its proximate cause is the reflective knowledge of one's own past actions.

Dependent and Non-Dependent Perfections

The ten perfections can be classed as either dependent or non-dependent. Dependent perfections may be either dependent on craving or dependent on wrong views.

> "Something carried out with a desire for a glorious future existence is said to be done dependent on craving. Something carried out in the mistaken belief that purification of defilements is achieved through morality is said to be done dependent on wrong views."
>
> (*Visuddhimagga*)

A deed of merit done with a desire for existence in a higher plane or glorious existence is dependent on craving and is not development of perfections. Here, wishing for human existence to fulfil the perfections, as in the cases of the bodhisattas Campeyya and Saṅkhapāla, the two Nāga Kings, cannot be called dependent.

Some people think, "The practices of charity and morality, or merely taking up the life of an ascetic, are sufficient in themselves for the removal of defilements; no further practice exists." They regard their view as perfect. They sometimes acquire merit, but they totally disregard the need for insight knowledge leading to the path and its fruition. Their merit is dependent on wrong views and does not count as a fulfilment of perfections. Theirs is the type of merit sought after by fakirs. These two kinds of dependent merit keep one trapped in the cycle of rebirth. They are not called perfections.

Two Classes of Non-Dependent Merits

> "There is such a thing as supramundane merit, there is also mundane merit which serves as a seed for supramundane merit."
> (*Visuddhimagga*)

Since Maung Thaw's question relates to merit that contributes to the perfections, supramundane merit need not be discussed; only non-dependent mundane types of merit or mundane merit as the basis for the supramundane need be discussed here.

Only volitional activities such as giving, morality, renunciation, wisdom, energy, patience, truthfulness, resolve, loving-kindness, and equanimity, carried out with a pure mind and not bent towards a glorious existence hereafter, nor inspired by mistaken views, but aimed squarely at the "yonder shore" of enlightenment, as detached as the open sky, are merits that amount to fulfilling the perfections.

These days it is quite common to hear such prayers as: "May we attain nibbāna; for such time as we might not have attained nibbāna, for that time may we be..." and so on. Such are the prayers a donor makes at his or her offering ceremony, aspiring for ever higher and more magnificent existences and a grand vista of worldly attainments in words every bit as pompous as those the head of the Saṅgha uses when he administers the prayers during the water-pouring ceremony. The result is that the word "*nibbāna*" is heard as a mere faint sound drowned by a welter of mundane wishes. Furthermore, it is the mundane aspect of the prayers that seems to have the most appeal. For we have such a splendid range of those wishing words, and what eloquence! In fact it was to discourage that sort of cat-scratching merit that the emphatic article *eva* (only) is used in the passage referred to above: *tasseva* = *tassa* + *eva* ("that only is"). Only that kind of mundane merit is what the Buddha approves of.

Q. Would you regard those deeds where the donor wishes for nibbāna, with other mundane attainments, as meritorious deeds?

A. Yes. However, I would say that those types of merit do not help to quicken the time to enlightenment.

Let me illustrate with a few relevant examples.

In the dark ages (i.e., when the Buddha's teaching had fallen silent) before the coming of Vipassī Buddha there lived two brothers who were sugarcane planters. The younger of them was to become Jotika, the celebrated rich man. They offered sugarcane juice to a Solitary Buddha. The elder brother, in making his wishes for the merit that would accrue from the gift, said, "May I know the Dhamma that the Solitary Buddha has known." The younger brother also said the same thing, and something more. He added his wishes for glorious existence—two common mundane wishes. The elder brother gained enlightenment at the earliest encounter with a Buddha, in this case Buddha Vipassī. As for the younger brother, because his desire was not "nibbāna specific" but went off at a tangent, he missed his chance for enlightenment under the teaching of Vipassī Buddha. He attained release from existence only under the teaching of Gotama Buddha, after having missed the teachings of six Buddhas.

The moral of the story is this: when you are doing some meritorious deed, do not let craving for future well-being enter your mind. If you allow it, your wishes are bound to become your shackles. For the greater your well-being, the stronger your craving is likely to be, so that you find yourself dilly-dallying when the opportunity for enlightenment comes. If you aspire just for supramundane merit unencumbered by mundane wishes, then you can probably forsake worldly glories when you hear the Dhamma. So, Maung Thaw, you should remember that when you aspire for human existence it should be only to fulfil the perfections, which are required for enlightenment. However, don't ever let your wishes wander away to mundane attainments or well-being.

There is also the story of Puṇṇa, a householder servant of Meṇḍaka the rich man, who had strong attachment to existence as his master's trusted servant. So, when he wished for the result of his offering to a Solitary Buddha, he opted for service under his good master in his future existences! Of course his wish was fulfilled—he became his master's servant throughout their remaining existences together.

When Cūḷa Subhaddā, the consort of the King of Elephants (the bodhisatta), wished for the result of offering fruits to a

Solitary Buddha, she sought revenge on her husband for an imagined slight she had suffered. Her desire was fulfilled in her next existence as a human queen when she successfully plotted the death of her husband of the previous existence. This spiteful deed sent her down to hell.

Kusa, the bodhisatta, and his consort, Pabhāvatī, both made offerings to a Solitary Buddha in one of their past existences. They had to go through a series of mishaps together because they made discordant wishes.

These are only a few instances of the life stories of misdirected aspiration while doing a deed of merit. Such stories abound in the Jātakas and in history and folklore. A lot depends on one's mentor too. In the life story of Vidhura, the wise counsellor, we find that of four rich men who offered food to four recluses of supernormal attainments in jhānic powers, one became a Nāga and one a Garuda, one became a great king and one became Sakka (king of Tāvatiṃsa heaven). This is because the first two were given bad counsel from their respective teachers. So, one must take great care in choosing a mentor; bad counsel can bring bitter consequences for one's actions quite undeservedly.

Low, Medium, and Superior Grades of Merit

For each of the ten meritorious practices such as giving, morality, renunciation, etc., there can be three grades: low, medium, or superior.

> "A deed undertaken out of desire for fame is low. One undertaken with desire for the fruits of merit is moderate. One undertaken with the clear understanding that it is the custom of the Noble Ones is superior."
>
> (*Visuddhimagga*)

Of the above three grades, the first is done for vanity, all for show. It hardly brings any merit that could result in future well-being, let alone fulfil any perfections. The second is motivated by desire for merit. Usually it is done with discrimination since the donor selects the most worthy recipient whenever possible to gain the greatest merit. This kind of deed brings ample results in the mundane spheres, but still does not amount to fulfilling a perfection. The third case is where one sets one's mind on the deed alone, not on its consequences. The donor is guided by a true sense of charity. In fact, one is prepared to share any of one's possessions with others, for one has no attachment to them. One rightly follows the practice of the Noble Ones. One does not choose to whom to give. Let anyone come, whether good, bad, or average, one would make some kind of gift. This kind of giving is following the custom of the Noble Ones. It is truly a practice for the perfection of giving. The same spirit of considering the deed alone, and not its rewards, governs the remaining perfections such as morality, renunciation, wisdom, energy, patience, truthfulness, etc.

Another way of classifying virtue is as follows:

> "Virtue observed out of craving for glorious existences and material well-being is inferior; virtue observed for one's own release is moderate; virtue observed to liberate all beings, which is the perfection of virtue, is superior."
>
> (*Visuddhimagga*)

Release from the cycle of birth and death, and release from the mundane attainments of glorious existences, mean the same thing. The second grade is regarded as inferior because it falls short of being a practice for perfections. Observance for the sake of one's own release is the perfection practised by the Solitary Buddhas and ordinary disciples. Observance for the liberation of all beings is the perfection practised by Perfectly Enlightened Buddhas.

The Perfections Explained

I shall now explain the meaning of each of the ten perfections:

1. *Dāna*: Giving, making a gift or offering. Sharing one's wealth unstintingly with virtuous disciples of the Buddha is called sharing, or the practice of common ownership. The bodhisatta's practice of making gifts to anyone, virtuous, unvirtuous, or

moderately virtuous, has already been mentioned. It means that anyone who calls at one's door for alms receives them. Herein, "virtuous disciples" means special people who deserve the enjoyment of one's wealth because they will share the knowledge of the Dhamma. With respect to such good people, sharing should take the form of respectful offerings after careful preparation.

2. *Sīla*: There are two kinds of morality; avoidance of the three bodily misdeeds and the four verbal misdeeds *(vārittasīla)*; and cultivating virtuous habits *(cārittasīla)*. The latter means paying respect *(apacāyana)* to the Buddha, Dhamma, and Saṅgha, and to parents, teachers, and those senior in age, status, or morality; or helping anyone with a meritorious deed as if it were one's own undertaking *(veyyāvacca)*.

3. *Nekkhamma*: Renunciation is undertaken with a strong volition of non-greed, therefore it is a meritorious deed. Even if a householder strives to dispel greed by contemplating the repulsiveness of the body or the loathsomeness of food, it amounts to renunciation, which is meritorious. If one can do more, one may go to a solitary retreat for the same purpose. If one can go a step further, one may become a recluse or, still better, a bhikkhu. Even better, one may take up the practice of concentration and gain the first jhāna. Better than this, one may develop insight to attain the path of non-returning. All these are the meritorious deeds of renunciation.

4. *Paññā*: Wisdom is of two kinds, mundane and supramundane. Learning the Tipiṭaka, and teaching it to others, undertaken to fulfil the perfection of wisdom, is supramundane. Teaching others the harmless sciences of astrology, incantations, recitation of verses, medicine, science; or the arts, such as mechanics, mathematics, painting, sculpture, metalwork, masonry, gold-smithery, ironmongery, etc., or honest ways of trade and agriculture and all such blameless vocations, are mundane. All these three categories, if imparted to others in a noble spirit as "perfection directed" acts, are the practice of the perfection of wisdom.

5. *Viriya*: Energy is supreme if it conforms to the four right efforts *(sammappadāna)*. Besides this, exerting one's utmost strength with a pure motive to help others, whether one is capable or not, also amounts to the perfection of energy.

6. *Khanti*: Patience is tolerating others and bearing unpleasant experiences such as cold and heat. The Buddha says, "Bearing the severity of cold, or bearing the severity of heat, thus one has patience." The Buddha goes on to explain patience in various other ways. The underlying quality of patience is placidity in the face of internal or external unpleasant experiences, coupled with fortitude. A man of patience does not allow anyone or anything "to put the grit in the machine." "Come wind, come foul weather," he goes about his meritorious routine, not with hedonistic indifference, but with an imperturbable heart, devoid of ill-will. The presence of such a tolerant frame of mind is patience.

7. *Sacca*: Truthfulness means avoidance of untruth and falsehood under all circumstances.

8. *Adhiṭṭhāna*: Resolve is the firmness of one's stand after one has committed oneself to something, whether expressed or not.

9. *Mettā*: Loving-kindness means wishing others well, with a heart filled with goodwill towards any being that one comes across.

10. *Upekkhā*: Equanimity is the quality of being strictly impartial to both well-wishers and adversaries alike. One does not behave partially towards one's benefactors. Neither does one harbour any resentment towards one's detractors. This evenness of attitude toward both the kind and the unkind is the essence of equanimity.

Here are a few similes to drive home the significance of the perfections. Patience and equanimity are the mainstay for the other perfections. Only when one has established these two can one expect to fulfil the rest. Just as a newborn infant can only survive with the care of its parents, the remaining eight perfections can only be fulfilled under the constant care of patience and equanimity. Patience may be likened to the mother and equanimity to the father.

If patience and equanimity are present, and the other good deeds are forthcoming under their benign influence, if there is an absence of renunciation, these good deeds will not properly become perfections. Lacking the guidance of renunciation, one is liable to be overcome by attachment to the merit derived from them and yearn for mundane benefits. Then the meritorious deeds merely prolong rebirth because they are dependent on existence. They do not then qualify as perfections. Therefore, if patience and equanimity are the parents, renunciation should be called the family doctor who takes care of the child's health.

To employ a different simile: all vegetation depends on soil and water for its survival; both must be favourable. Similarly, patience provides the favourable soil, and equanimity the favourable water, for the remaining perfections.

Equanimity in the present context is slightly different from the equanimity of the four divine abidings *(brahmavihārā)*, which signifies impartiality to the welfare of all beings (different from being uninterested). Equanimity as perfection is evenness of mind regarding one who worships you and one who condemns or persecutes you and, further, being able to seek the welfare of both.

How the Perfections are Practised Together

In one of the innumerable existences of the bodhisatta, he was born as a monkey chieftain. A brahmin lost his way in the forest and fell into a chasm that was as deep as the height of a hundred men. Seeing his plight, the bodhisatta took pity on him and exerted himself to rescue him. Eventually, the brahmin was carried up onto safe ground. The bodhisatta was, by then, quite exhausted, so he fell asleep, unsuspectingly, on the brahmin's lap. The brahmin thought to himself, "I've earned nothing today. My wife is going to be upset when I get home. What a delightful idea if I were to bring home monkey flesh. How pleased my wife would be!" Satisfied with his "bright idea," the brahmin took up a stone lying nearby and dealt a blow to the monkey's head. It was such a vicious blow that blood gushed out of the wound in all directions. Stupefied and covered in blood, the bodhisatta leapt up into a tree. He could not believe that such a thing could happen! "Oh, there are such people in this world." Then the thought came to his mind how to lead the man home safely, for the forest was full of leopards, tigers, and other dangerous animals. He said to the brahmin, "Now you should be starting for home. I must show you the way out of this forest, but I cannot trust you. You can follow the trail of my blood as I jump from tree to tree." So, in this way the brahmin got home safely.

In this Jātaka it will be seen that loving-kindness was the first of the ten perfections that the bodhisatta practised. When he saw the plight of the brahmin he took pity on him as if he were his own son and started thinking of how to save him. Assessing the situation and devising a plan to take the brahmin out from the chasm was wisdom. Executing the plan at great risk to himself, and using all his strength, was the practice of energy. In bearing the deadly injury that had broken his skull, without getting angry, he exercised great patience. Without it he would have left the ungrateful man, thereby rendering all his efforts futile. Not allowing himself to be overcome by anger for such a wicked deed was the practice of equanimity. Had he not been firm in the practice of equanimity, he might have left off there, and the heartless brahmin would not have survived long. Indeed the two principal perfections of patience and equanimity saw through the whole undertaking.

Saving the brahmin from such a deep chasm at the risk of his life amounted to sacrifice of his life or generosity. Again, saving the brahmin's life was the gift of life. Not even uttering a curse, and never raising his hand to strike back, constituted morality. In doing this noble deed the bodhisatta never thought about the merit he would gain. That was renunciation, the ability to forsake all forms of existence. For attachment to a better life hereafter is generally strong enough to spoil the perfection of renunciation. By not going back on his word to save the brahmin, the bodhisatta accomplished truthfulness—not very easy to keep under the circumstances. Lastly, fulfilling his commitment without wavering in spite of the brahmin's shocking treatment, was resolve. This was how the bodhisatta successfully practised the ten perfections in a single undertaking.

Regarding your particular interest in the aspiration to Buddhahood, this is a fairly wide subject. The detailed process of laying the foundation for the aspiration to, and the fulfilment of, Perfect Enlightenment is dealt with in the scriptures in fifteen catechisms. Only a brief account will be given here. For a wider knowledge on it, please see the Cariyāpiṭaka Commentary and the Sīlakkhandha Subcommentary.

The Three Grades of Perfections

I shall now outline the ten ordinary perfections, the ten higher perfections, and the ten supreme perfections.

All external objects such as a wife and children, animate and inanimate things, belonging to a person, are the objects through which the ten ordinary perfections are fulfilled. One's own limbs or head or any organs of the body are the objects through which the ten higher perfections are fulfilled. One's own life (being sacrificed) is the object through which the ten supreme perfections are fulfilled.

Of those three categories of objects, undertakings that forsake the first category are called ordinary perfections. Undertakings that forsake the second are called higher perfections. Those that forsake the third, i.e. one's own life, are called supreme perfections.

One who can fulfil only the first ten attains the enlightenment of a Noble Disciple. One who can fulfil only the first ten and the second ten attains the enlightenment of a Solitary Buddha. One who can fulfil all thirty attains Supreme Self-Enlightenment.

The Three Types of Disciples' Enlightenment

There are three classes of enlightenment of a Noble Disciple: (i) an Ordinary Noble Disciple's, (ii) a Great Disciple's, and (iii) a Chief Disciple's. By fulfilling the first ten perfections for one aeon and a hundred thousand world cycles, one can attain the enlightenment of a Chief Disciple. By the Chief Disciples are meant the Buddha's two principal Noble Disciples like the Venerables Sāriputta and Moggallāna for Gotama Buddha.

By fulfilling the same perfections for a hundred thousand world cycles, one can attain the enlightenment of a Great Disciple. By the Great Disciples are meant the distinguished Noble Ones, numbering eighty for Buddha Gotama.

There is no mention of the duration for the maturity of an ordinary Noble Disciple. One has to infer it from such statements as are found in certain commentaries. In a commentary on the Arahants' supernormal power of recollecting former existences, an ordinary Noble One is said to be able to recall existences from a hundred to a thousand world cycles. This has generally been taken as the maturity period for an ordinary Noble Disciple.

Once, a frog was accidentally killed while listening with rapt attention to the mellifluous voice of the Buddha preaching. He was reborn as a deva from the merit of listening attentively to the Dhamma (even though he did not understand its meaning). Immediately, he came to pay homage to the Buddha, listened to his discourse, and gained stream-winning. In his next existence he became an Arahant. From this story we can see that there are just a few forms of existence in which a disciple's enlightenment is attained.

Regarding the Chief and Great Disciples, the periods for maturity stated earlier refer only to the periods after these Noble Ones had received formal recognition by a living Buddha. The Buddha predicts when, where, and under what circumstances he will attain which type of enlightenment. This is called "receiving the word" *(vyākaraṇa)*.

The scriptures are silent on the duration for fulfilling the perfections before such recognition or assurance. The interval between the arising of any two Buddhas is beyond reckoning. It may be any number of world cycles. A Noble Disciple (as the term signifies) can arise only when a Buddha arises or his teaching is extant. So it is important to remember that those durations mentioned above refer only to those Noble Ones who encountered Gotama Buddha.

As to the Noble Disciples: in the commentary on the Suttanipāta there are three types: (i) one who depends on confidence for his enlightenment, (ii) one who depends on diligence, and (iii) one who depends on wisdom.

The Three Types of Solitary Enlightenment

Similarly, Solitary Enlightenment *(paccekabodhi)* is also of three types. The commentaries say that the enlightenment of a Solitary Buddha is attained after fulfilling the ten perfections and the ten higher perfections for two aeons and a hundred thousand world cycles.

The Three Types of Perfect Enlightenment

The Perfect Enlightenment of a Buddha is also of these three types, which are also called: (i) *ugghātitaññūbodhi*, (ii) *vipañcita-ññūbodhi*, and (iii) *ñeyyabodhi* respectively.

A Buddha who depends on wisdom for his enlightenment, after receiving the assurance, has to fulfil the ten perfections, the ten higher perfections, and the ten supreme perfections for four aeons and a hundred thousand world cycles.

A Buddha who depends on diligence must fulfil the perfections for eight aeons and a hundred thousand world cycles.

A Buddha who depends on confidence must fulfil the perfections for sixteen aeons and a hundred thousand world cycles.

This is what has been recorded in the ancient commentaries. However, there are differing views regarding the maturity periods for the three types of Buddhas. They are found in later works such as the Apadāna Commentary and in subcommentaries such as *Sotattakī, Tathāgatuppatti, Mahāvaṃsaṭīkā*, etc.

On this controversial subject an analogy given by the commentator on the Suttanipāta is worth noting. He says that trees and plants require a certain time before they can flower or bear fruit. Trees like the tamarind or the jack-fruit tree will not mature to blossom or bear fruit in one, two, or three years however carefully one nurtures them, even by watering a hundred times a day. Similarly, with the fulfilment of the prerequisites for Buddhahood. Let one give daily offerings on the scale of King Vessantara[1] to fulfil the perfections, one cannot attain Buddhahood any sooner.

The periods for maturity necessarily vary for each of the three types of Buddhas (see the Suttanipāta Commentary).

1 See Vessantara Jātaka, Jātaka No.547.

The Noblest Aspiration

What is meant by the Noblest Aspiration *(mahābhinīhāra)* should be understood. The foundation *(mūla)*, condition *(paccaya)*, and the root cause *(hetu)* of the Noblest Aspiration should be understood. Mahābodhi should be understood. Its foundation, condition, and root cause should be understood.

What is meant by "the Noblest Aspiration"? It is the verbal and mental undertaking that the bodhisatta had made at some point of time aeons before taking up the perfections.

It was made in these terms:

> "As a man who knows his own strength, what use is there to get to 'the yonder shore' (nibbāna) alone? I will attain to Supreme Knowledge and then convey men and devas to the yonder shore."

That was the pledge that sent the ten thousand universes reeling and echoing in applause. That was the bodhisatta's earnest wish. For he intensely aspired to Supreme Self-Enlightenment thus:

> "Knowing the Truth, I will let others know it. Freeing myself from the world, I will free others. Having crossed over, I will enable others to cross."

This fervent and most daring aspiration is called "the Noblest Aspiration."

Eight Factors Needed for the Noblest Aspiration

For the Noblest Aspiration to materialize, eight factors must be present:

> *"Manussattaṃ liṅgasampatti, hetu satthāradassanaṃ.*
> *Pabbajjā guṇasampatti, adhikāroca chandatā.*
> *Aṭṭhadhammasamodhānā, abhinīhāro samijjhati."*
>
> *(atthasālinī; Buddhavaṃsa.)*

1. The aspirant must be a human being *(manussattaṃ)*.
2. He must be a man *(liṅgasampatti)*.
3. His spiritual maturity must be sufficient to attain Arahantship if he chose to (root-condition, *hetu*).
4. He must have met a living Buddha *(satthāradassanaṃ)*.
5. He must have taken up the life of a recluse or a monk *(pabbajjā)*.
6. He must have attained supernormal powers through concentration *(guṇasampatti)*.
7. He must have made the utmost homage *(adhikāro)* to the "Three Gems" while aspiring to Buddhahood.
8. He must have a most ardent will to become a Buddha *(chandatā)*.

If all eight factors are present, the Noblest Aspiration materializes. Herein "root-condition" means the four conditions *(paccaya)* and the four root causes *(hetu)*, which will be explained a little later.

Adhikāro means offerings, including his own life.

Chanda means a burning desire amounting to will or resolve, a preparedness for any eventuality. For example, suppose the entire universe was covered with sharp-pointed spikes, and suppose it was certain one could attain Buddhahood only by crossing it, the bodhisatta would never hesitate to cross it. Or suppose this universe was filled with glowing charcoal, the bodhisatta would not have wavered.

These are the illustrations given in the commentaries. In the commentary on the Khadiraṅgāra Jātaka, it is said that if the bodhisatta tried to cross, those steel spikes would turn into a vast stretch of rubies (in respectful recognition of his sincerity and resolve). Likewise, the burning charcoal would turn into a sea of lotus flowers.

Of those eight opportune factors, the ardent wish of a Solitary Buddha is attended by three factors: (i) meeting with a living Buddha, (ii) making the utmost reverence while declaring the wish for Solitary Buddhahood, and (iii) the will to become a Solitary Buddha.

For the enlightenment of a disciple three factors are needed: (i) meeting with a Solitary Buddha or an Arahant, (ii) making the utmost reverence while making the wish for the enlightenment of a disciple, and (iii) the will to become an Arahant.

The Two Root-Conditions

Root-condition, the third factor of the eight, means a bodhisatta aspiring to Buddhahood must be spiritually mature. When aspiring for Buddhahood in the presence of the Buddha, to receive the assurance he must have sufficient perfections to attain Solitary Buddhahood or Arahantship. He must then possess two further qualifications:

1. *Karuṇāsampatti*—great compassion,
2. *Upāyakosallasampatti*—skilful means.

Only when these two are present will a bodhisatta be duly recognized by the Buddha from whom he is to receive the assurance. By great compassion is meant great kindness and compassion for others that takes precedence over his own life. "Skilful means" is the genius that is equal to the task whenever he undertakes to help others. Literally, it is the "attainment of special aptitude in strategy." These two are the conditions for the (now specific) undertaking of the perfections that will suffice for the declaration of the Noblest Aspiration.

The Four Conditions

There are four further conditions *(paccaya)*, also called the four stages of maturity *(Buddhabhūmi)*, necessary to qualify as a bodhisatta:

1. *Ussāha*—exceptional energy;
2. *Ummaṅga*—a keen intellect;
3. *Avaṭṭhāna*—steadfastness of purpose;
4. *Hitacariyā*——compassion, loving-kindness for others, even outweighing one's own welfare.

The Four Root Causes

There are four root causes: 1) attainment of sufficient perfections *(upanissayasampatti)*, 2) attainment of compassion *(karuṇ-ajjhā-*

sayasampatti), 3) attainment of fortitude *(avihaññasampatti)*, and 4) attainment of good friendship *(kalyāṇamittasampatti)*.

1. Attainment of sufficient perfections means having sufficient perfections to attain Arahantship or Solitary Buddhahood at the time of the assurance.

2. Attainment of compassion is the endowment with a compassionate heart or universal loving-kindness.

3. Attainment of fortitude is a natural disposition for helping others. It is the abiding disposition that never tires in fulfilling the perfections. A luxurious life in the celestial realms is boring to a bodhisatta because it does not offer any opportunity to fulfil the perfections, particularly in serving others. Literally, *avihañña* means "never being vexed." It also implies spiritedness. The duration necessary for the maturity of the perfections ranges from four aeons and a hundred thousand world cycles to sixteen aeons and a hundred thousand world cycles, yet the spirit of a bodhisatta is such that he feels he is going to reach maturity the next day. In other words, he is already anticipating Buddhahood that is forthcoming only at the end of such staggering periods. No duration is too long for him to wait.

4. Attainment of good friendship is care and respect in attending to the wise in all his existences, whether human or celestial.

The Natural Inclinations of a Bodhisatta

A bodhisatta is further endowed with six natural inclinations:

1. Inclination to non-greed—a bodhisatta instinctively sees the danger in greed;
2. Inclination to non-hatred—a bodhisatta instinctively sees the danger in hatred or anger;
3. Inclination to non-delusion—a bodhisatta instinctively sees the danger in delusion;
4. Inclination to renunciation—a bodhisatta instinctively sees the danger in sensuality;
5. Inclination to seclusion—a bodhisatta instinctively sees the danger in socializing;
6. Inclination to escape from the cycle of rebirth—a bodhisatta instinctively sees the danger in existence.

The Significance of the Natural Inclinations

Just as the pith makes a tree durable, the six inclinations make a bodhisatta durable or steadfast. One who has these six inclinations, though living in the world, is like a water-container made of a dried gourd, which has no mouth, immersed in deep water. A person lacking them is like an earthen water pot with a wide mouth immersed in deep water. Even among lay people there are those in whom these six inclinations are present. They are like a water-gourd immersed in deep water. On the other hand, even among bhikkhus, there are those who lack these six inclinations. They are like a wide-mouthed water pot immersed in shallow water. The sensuous world of lay people is like deep water; the favourable facilities that the bhikkhus enjoy, such as secure monasteries, well-made furniture, fine utensils, and nutritious food, etc., are like shallow water.

1. Those who have no inclination to non-greed do not like to listen to talk on dispelling greed. Even trifling possessions oppress them like a heavy mountain. To those having a strong inclination to non-greed, the glories of a Universal Monarch are not worth a straw.

2. Those who have no inclination to non-hatred do not like to listen to advice on dispelling anger. The slightest provocation will infuriate them, just like a spark falling on dry grass or leaves. However, those firm in their inclination to non-hatred soon dispel any anger, even if they are wronged by a gross injustice, just as a fire brand that falls on a stack of green timber does not start a fire.

3. Those who have no inclination to non-delusion do not like to listen to talk on wisdom. They never see even a glimmer of the light of the Dhamma, which has a luminosity of eighty-four thousand candlepower, so to speak. They are shrouded in dark delusion regarding the real nature of the five aggregates. Living in darkness, they die in the dark and let one existence after another go to waste. The darkness of their delusion is just like congenital blindness. How could one born blind ever see light even if eighty-four thousand suns were to shine forth together?

4. Those who have no inclination to renunciation do not like to listen to talk on the advantages of renouncing worldly life. Their attachment to the fruit of their meritorious deeds such as giving,

virtue, or keeping the eight precepts, prevents those deeds from becoming perfections. Attachment corrupts them just as fungus spoils the choicest seeds set apart for cultivation, or as viruses, locusts, and other pests render a well-planted field infertile.

5. Those who have no inclination to seclusion do not like to listen to advice on seeking a solitary life in the forest. They are unable to tear themselves away from society for a quiet moment alone. Desire for companionship always pulls them into shallow friendships and ensures that they remain there, like a prisoner guarded by jailors.

6. Those who have no inclination to escape from the cycle of rebirth do not like to listen to advice on the emptiness of worldly life. They are under the serfdom of attachment to existence. That attachment does not allow them to aspire after the higher practice of the Dhamma leading to path knowledge. Instead, it keeps them satisfied with their parochial interests such as throwing lavish feasts, building pagodas, or donating monasteries and rest-houses. They are content with keeping the precepts, or remaining as devout laity, or as recluses or bhikkhus with virtue, or with some shallow achievement like teaching the Dhamma or writing books. These are only merits that hold them fast to the world, the wholesome kamma that prolongs existence. It is like the British Raj, which allowed their colonial subjects to enter freely into small businesses but would not tolerate any dealing with weapons, for fear of rebellion.

Herein, two kinds of attachment to existence should be known: yearning for some better existence hereafter, and a fond attachment to the present existence. The present existence offers a precious chance to attain nibbāna. The Tipiṭaka abounds in practical instructions showing the way to nibbāna. It is only because so-called Buddhists are enamoured of the present existence, and are pampering their little bodies, that they fight shy of the stringent discipline demanded to gain enlightenment. It is a pity they cannot gain even some concentration, which recluses of ancient times gained without the benefit of the Buddha's teaching.

The Four Special Characteristics of a Bodhisatta

I shall now deal with the four special characteristics of a bodhisatta that distinguish him from a future Solitary Buddha. They are glaringly obvious as if they were garlands around his neck.

1. *Indriya*—the five controlling faculties. Unshakable confidence *(saddhā)*, indefatigable diligence *(viriya)*, unwavering mindfulness *(sati)*, steadfast concentration *(samādhi)*, and unerring wisdom *(paññā)* are the first mark that distinguishes a bodhisatta.

2. *Paṭipatti*—the practice. A bodhisatta is always out to help others and places the welfare of others before his own. He never expects any return for the efforts he makes for others' welfare. Nor will he care to mention them, whether in his beneficiary's presence or not. Even if the beneficiary "bites the hand that feeds," a bodhisatta never turns back from any good deed. This holds true even when his life is in imminent danger. This is the bodhisatta's sense of wishing well for the present. Regarding merits accruing from his noble deeds in giving or in cultivating virtue, etc., a bodhisatta sets his sights higher than the solitary attainment of nibbāna. He aims only at supreme enlightenment, by which he can show the way to nibbāna. This is a bodhisatta's practice for the hereafter. This twofold practice also distinguishes a bodhisatta.

3. *Kosalla*—proficiency. This is manifested in sound reasoning *(cintāmayañāṇa)* and presence of mind *(taṅkhaṇuppattiñāṇa)* that never fail him. Though the future disciples or Solitary Buddhas also have these two intellectual qualities to a high degree, they are liable to err occasionally. With the bodhisatta, these two qualities are unerring. This is the proficiency of a bodhisatta that makes him unique among other aspirants to enlightenment.

4. *Ajjhāsaya*—inclination. The texts treat this subject quite comprehensively concerning the perfections, but I shall describe it only briefly. Regarding giving, for example, a bodhisatta is very happy in making gifts. Whenever he has something to offer as a gift and a recipient is not available, he feels frustrated. Whenever he gives, he gives it with a light heart, and takes proper care in doing so. No amount of giving would satisfy his zeal for charity. Whenever anybody asks anything of him, he does not judge him by class or creed but always complies gladly. In doing so, he never

thinks of his own needs but gives to satisfy the other's needs only. Refer to the Buddhavaṃsa on this, particularly the passage beginning: *"Yathāpi kumbho sampuṇṇo..."* [2]

In that passage, which is from the chapter on the perfection of generosity, "inclination" is described thus:

"As when one overturns a large cooking pot filled with oil or buttermilk to empty it, not a drop or even the dregs remain, but runs out of the pot, so also when a bodhisatta makes an offering... Whether the beggar is a filthy blockhead of a labourer with bovine instincts, or a drunkard, or better than them, a man who has taken refuge in the Three Gems, or one who keeps the five precepts; or in brief, whether he is good, average, or bad, let him come for alms at any time, the bodhisatta never judges what type of fellow he is, or whether it is worth giving him so much or anything at all; but never discriminating, never hesitating, [he gives freely]."

Of the different classes of beggars ranging from wretched to excellent, the bodhisatta never bothers sizing up a person who calls at the door for some help or alms. The amount he gives is also not dependent on the class of beggar. This kind of completely indiscriminate offering is another characteristic of a bodhisatta.

In respect of the nine remaining perfections, this example on giving should be applied with due alteration of details. Those not conversant with Pāḷi can get the essence of what the text says from the passage quoted above.

These days there are some who wish for Buddhahood, and wisdom-oriented Buddhahood at that, though their conduct barely qualifies them to become ordinary disciples. What characterizes them is the bold banner of craving-dependent deeds, which cry out for public recognition right now and yearn for glorious results hereafter.

"Who ever does something for nothing?" these people are apt to protest. "To expect good results from a good deed is only natural." But remember, a thing done without expecting future rewards brings a greater reward than is imagined. More signifi-

---

2 See p.16, §118 of the PTS edition under "Dīpaṅkarabuddhavaṃso," p.315 of the Burmese Chaṭṭhasaṅgītipiṭaka under "Sumedhapatthanākathā," or Vol.33, p.481 of the new Thai Dayyaraṭṭhassa Saṅgītitepiṭaka. For an English translation see Sacred Books of the Buddhists, Vol.XXI, p.20, §§118-120.

cantly, it amounts to the real practice of the perfections essential for enlightenment. A meritorious deed done with an ardent wish for good results brings relatively limited results and does not amount to fulfilling the perfections. Remember the example of fungus in seed-grain or pests in a plantation.

Some say that gradual maturity is the likely process, for enlightenment right now is not possible. So why should one not store up merit for better existences and greater prosperity? My reply is this:

Small plants thrive just during the rainy season. Only one in a thousand or ten thousand among them might survive the long, dry, hot months till the next rainy season. Such a rare plant must be extraordinarily robust and hardy to have struck its main root deep enough. Such rare plants obviously need not fear the severity of the climate after having passed three or four rainy seasons.

By the same analogy, to achieve budding perfections is only possible when the Buddha's teaching is still extant. Whatever little perfection one has achieved during this opportune period has very little chance of surviving to be developed in the time of the next Buddha. Those sham deeds of merit will certainly lose their potential once the teaching has disappeared. Very few could survive the uncertainties of the intervening dark ages. During those dark ages, right view is lost to humanity and wrong views prevail. One who has acquired only sham deeds of merit falls into wrong views, and so their little potential of merit is soon gone. Imagine the fate of one who repeatedly falls into wrong view for two, three, or more existences. This is the unstable nature of the merits of a person who has not struck roots deep down, who has not attained stability. Such perishing of budding merits is the rule with most beings. Innumerable existences have already passed in which they acquired some flimsy merits, only to be lost again by the next existence. This process of acquisition and perishing goes on in perpetuity for the overwhelming majority of beings. This is why the idea of "gradual maturity" does not hold. It would be a great pity if one depends on such a mistaken idea and goes on hoping for the perfections while actually longing for the inexorable cycle of rebirth.

The four conditions, the four root causes, and the six inclinations are the factors for declaring the Noblest Aspiration and for taking up the higher perfections.

On declaring the Noblest Aspiration and receiving the assurance of future Buddhahood, the bodhisatta at once becomes endowed with the five powers *(bala)*, the four special characteristics, the two qualifications of compassion *(karuṇā)* and skill in strategy *(upāyakosalla)*, the four stages of maturity *(bhūmi)*, the six inclinations *(ajjhāsaya)*, etc. However, since what I have said so far should suffice to answer Maung Thaw's question I shall not deal with any further details.

Chapter Two

Maung Thaw's second question relates to the following:

1. The definition, characteristics, and significance of the five aggregates;
2. The definition, characteristics, and significance of the four truths;
3. A description of the five aggregates in terms of the four truths;
4. The definition, characteristics, and significance of the Noble Eightfold Path, with its practical application leading to nibbāna.

Seven Aspects of Materiality to be Perceived

There are two approaches to the definition, characteristics, and significance of the five aggregates, namely, the Suttanta method and the Abhidhamma method.

The Suttanta method is the Buddha's approach to the Dhamma for the ordinary person. The Buddha gave succinct discourses to show ordinary people practical ways to cultivate insight, and to attain the path and its fruition in this very life.

The Abhidhamma method, however, offers a profound and exhaustive analytical treatment of all aspects of the Dhamma, with no particular reference to the practice for insight development. The latter method is actually meant for the Noble Ones to sharpen their analytical knowledge *(paṭisambhidā-ñāṇa)*. It is not suitable as insight training for the ordinary person because it is too subtle. For example, those who have small boats should only ply the river for their livelihood and should not venture out to the deep ocean. Only if they have ocean-going vessels should they make an ocean voyage.

These days, people take up the holy life not actually intent on gaining path knowledge, but merely to acquire merit, purported to gradually mature as perfections. Practice of insight meditation is not popular. Learning and teaching of scriptures to develop wisdom is the usual practice. So the Abhidhamma method is popular. In this treatise, however, I shall employ the Suttanta method only.

"Bhikkhus, a bhikkhu who earnestly wants to understand the true nature of materiality to eradicate the defilements, who habitually contemplates materiality from three approaches, who is proficient in the seven aspects of materiality is, in this Dhamma and Discipline, called accomplished, one who has lived the life, a perfect one or an excellent man.

"Bhikkhus, how is a bhikkhu proficient in the seven aspects? Bhikkhus, herein a bhikkhu discerns the true nature of materiality; he discerns the origin of materiality; he discerns the cessation of materiality; he discerns the practice leading to the cessation of materiality; he discerns the satisfaction in materiality; he discerns the danger in materiality; and he discerns the escape from materiality.

"Bhikkhus, what is materiality? Materiality includes the four primary elements: extension, cohesion, heat, and motion, and the [twenty-four] material qualities derived from them. This is called materiality. (1)

"As long as nutriment arises, materiality arises. Once nutriment is exhausted, materiality ceases. This is the origin and cessation of materiality. (2, 3)

"What is the practice leading to the cessation of materiality? It is the Noble Eightfold Path taught by me: right view, right thought, right speech, right action, right livelihood, right effort, right mindfulness, and right concentration. These eight constitute the path. (4)

"The pleasure and joy arising dependent on materiality constitute the satisfaction in materiality. (5)

"The transience, unsatisfactoriness, and instability of materiality constitute the danger in materiality. (6)

"The abandonment of desire and lust for materiality constitute the escape from materiality." (7)

(*Sattaṭṭhāna Sutta, Khandhavagga, Saṃyuttanikāya*)

The True Nature of Materiality

1. The four essential material qualities are the primary elements of extension, cohesion, heat, and motion.
2. The five sense bases are the eye, the ear, the nose, the tongue, and the body.
3. The five sense objects are visible form, sound, smell, taste, and touch.
4. The two material qualities of sex are femininity and masculinity.
5. The material quality of vitality.
6. The material base of consciousness—the heart-base.
7. The material quality of nutrition.

These are the eighteen kinds of materiality.

1. The Four Primary Elements

i. The different degrees of hardness or softness are qualities of the element of extension, colloquially called the earth element.
ii. Liquidity and cohesion are qualities of the element of cohesion, colloquially called the water element.
iii. Temperature, hot or cold, is the quality of the element of heat, colloquially called the fire element.
iv. Motion, swelling, inflation, pressure, and support are qualities of the element of motion, colloquially called the wind element.

Due to the collective concept people usually conceive the four primary elements as a composite whole rather than in their ultimate sense, which can only be discerned through insight knowledge. When insight arises, one sees that not the tiniest atom remains that is compact or solid.

The three elements of extension, motion, and heat can be felt by touch. Even children know whether a thing is soft or hard. However, they are not able to discern the ultimate sense of what they only superficially recognize as the earth element. They know whether a thing is cold or hot, but they cannot discern the ultimate sense of what they only recognize as the fire element. Similarly they know that something moves, or supports, or is pressed, or swells. However, they do not discern the element of motion there. If one can penetrate conceptions about the four primary elements and realize their ultimate nature, then one is said to be proficient in materiality, the first aspect of discernment.

2. The Five Sense Bases

The eye, ear, nose, and tongue are the sense bases through which the respective kinds of sense-consciousness arises. Body-sensitivity has for its basis the whole body externally and internally. These are the kamma-conditioned material qualities or internal sense bases.

3. The Five Sense Objects

The five sense objects should need no explanation. Only that of touch may be commented on as that pertaining to the primary elements of extension, heat, and motion.[3] These three primary elements are the tangible sense objects.

4. The Material Qualities of Sex

i. The material quality of femininity, which governs a person's whole body, distinguishing her as a woman or imparting the condition of being female.
ii. The material quality of masculinity, which governs a person's whole body, distinguishing him as a man or imparting the condition of being male.

3 The element of cohesion cannot be touched. If you put your hand in water, you can know it is hot or cold, and you can feel its pressure. If you pick up a handful' you can feel its weight. If you hit the surface of water with your hand, you can feel its hardness. However, you cannot feel its cohesion *(ed.)*

5. *Vitality*

The vitality that gives a being its life, or the vitality of the kamma-originated materiality, that pervades the whole body.

6. *The Material Base of Consciousness*

The material base of consciousness or the mind is called the heart-base. It is the source from which kind thoughts or unkind thoughts flow.

7. *The Material Quality of Nutrition*

The material quality that nourishes the whole body, which may be called the sustenance of the four primary elements, is the element of nutrition. The principle underlying this element is the need of all beings born in the sensual realm to eat. It is just like an oil-lamp that needs constant replenishment to be kept alight.[4]

Of the eighteen material qualities mentioned above, the four primary elements are like the roots, the trunk, the boughs, and the branches of a tree; the remaining fourteen are like the leaves, flowers, and fruits. When the impermanence of the four primary elements is perceived, the delusion of personality disappears. Derived materiality does not then obstruct perception. That, it should be noted, is why the Buddha speaks of the four great primaries but does not define them. These four primary elements are self-evident.

All materiality, whether animate or inanimate, can be reduced to atoms. On further analysis, they are included in one of the eighteen species of material qualities. Contemplate your own body to gain insight. If the ultimate materiality in the four primary elements is perceived clearly, the infinite materiality of the universe will be seen in the same light. Therefore, contemplate hard on the four primary elements.

Derived material phenomena are not so evident, for they are interrelated and subtle. Examine what is already evident; do not try to see what is imperceptible. It will only be a waste of effort.

---

4 Pāli phraseology makes heavy reading and usually fails to communicate, so I shall use everyday Burmese to explain abstract matters. [Author's Note]

Focus your attention on only one of the four primary elements. Once any one of them is perceived clearly, the remaining three will also become clear.

This body is a composite of ultimate realities, i.e. of things having their individual essence. Just as a person with weak eyesight has to use glasses to read, use the Buddha's teaching as an aid to see the ultimate truth that is clearly visible inside your body. Try to see the arising and vanishing that is constantly taking place within you. With sufficient zeal and concentration you can probably comprehend things quite vividly. I am impressing it on you in various ways because it is elusive.

This first aspect needs to be properly perceived whereby the primary elements become clear in their ultimate sense, without confusing them with the collective concept. One cannot stress this too strongly because the remaining aspects will not be discerned unless you have the first one well and truly within your grasp. So spare no pains to perceive it.

The Origin and Cessation of Materiality

These are the second and third aspects to be perceived. Constant arising is called "*samudaya.*" Cessation or vanishing, is called "*nirodha.*" *Samudaya* is used in two senses: first to refer to the constant arising of phenomena throughout a given existence; and second to refer to the arising of another existence when the present one ends.

Nirodha is also used in two senses: the constant cessation of phenomena throughout a given existence, and the final cessation of all phenomena when one attains parinibbāna, where there is no more fresh existence and one escapes from the cycle of rebirth. This is also called *nibbāna nirodha*.

Nutriment *(āhāra)* is the sustenance of existence. It is of two kinds: physical nutriment and mental nutriment. Physical nutriment is the material quality of nutrition. Mental nutriment means contact, volition, and consciousness.

> "The past kamma that accompanies one throughout the cycle of rebirth is comparable to a field, rebirth-consciousness is like the seed-grain, the craving that accompanies kamma is

like the fertility of the soil—*kammaṃ khettaṃ viññāṇaṃ bījaṃ taṇhā sineho.*"

In the above quotation, kamma is the mental nutriment of volition, rebirth-consciousness is the nutriment of consciousness, which provides the seed for a new existence at rebirth, leading to a new material aggregate, i.e. the body.

In lighting a candle, the light appears simultaneously with the flame. Similarly, at rebirth, materiality appears the instant that rebirth-consciousness arises. The earliest appearance of materiality is like the germination of the seed. Our full-grown bodies are the natural development from rebirth-consciousness like the seed that has germinated and grown into a tree. It should be understood that germination can occur only where there is rebirth-consciousness. If the rebirth-consciousness does not arise when a person dies with the exhaustion of the past kamma, there is no germination. That is what is meant by the Buddha's words:

"When nutrition arises, materiality arises. When nutrition is exhausted, materiality ceases."

This is the explanation of the second meaning of *samudaya*, the incessant rebirth of new aggregates of materiality. Similarly with *nirodha*, the cessation of rebirth, the total release from the cycle of rebirths. This second sense of arising and cessation is obvious. This is not vital for the development of insight. What is relevant here is to know the constant arising and cessation taking place every moment throughout one's life.

Here is a simile: Let us say a man-size flame is set alight and is meant to last a hundred years. Imagine how much fuel must be supplied every day and night. The life of the flame depends on the fuel. The flame can remain the size of a man only when the lamp is full. It becomes smaller as the fuel level falls. When the oil is used up, the flame goes out. Imagine how much fuel is consumed by the lamp each day from the first day it is lit. Visualize the daily refuelling. Then consider how the flame gets renewed because the fuel is replenished. See how the flame exhausts itself due to the exhaustion of the fuel that has kept it alight. Try to distinguish the rejuvenated flame, after refuelling, from the flame that has exhausted itself, having consumed all the fuel. Suppose that the new fuel is coloured, and that the flame takes on the same colour as the fuel. For a while, white fuel will produce a white flame. Then as the white fuel is used up, and red fuel is fed into the lamp, the colour of the flame will turn from white to red. Again, with yellow fuel, the flame turns yellow, and so on. Thus, compare the old and the new in the same flame.

Preconceived notions about what the eye sees obstruct perception. Expel these preconceptions with insight. Even in an ordinary flame (not distinguished by colour) constant change is observable if one looks closely. Every motion represents change—change from the old to the new. As the new arises, the old vanishes. The arising of the new must be understood as samudaya—the vanishing of the old is *nirodha*.

The temperature-originated materiality that is the body, which will remain when a person dies, is just like the lamp and the wick in our simile. The kamma-originated materiality, the consciousness-originated materiality, and the nutriment-originated materiality, which combine to give the illusion of a person, are like the man-size flame. The daily food intake is like the daily refuelling.

Our body gets the calories it needs from the food that we take. As the food gets assimilated, the fine materiality in our body gets reduced. When food intake is discontinued and nutrition is exhausted, the fine materiality and the kamma-originated materiality that constitute the body cease to function. All the different physical phenomena that constitute the body are totally dependent on nutrition. The exhaustion of nutrition from the previous meal and the cessation of the older materiality go together, just as they had arisen together. The arising of nutrition from a later meal and the arising of the new materiality also coincide.

If you contemplate the enormous struggle of all living beings to obtain food, you will realize the startling rate at which materiality changes in all living things. Then the manner in which one sustains oneself from the moment of birth, seeking to extend one's life with food, will become evident. As one can visualize the changing colours of the flame after refuelling with different fuel, try to visualize the exhaustion of a fresh meal's nutriment with the consequent changes in materiality. Focus on the changes that take place from moment to moment. The arising of fresh materiality as you eat, and the feeling of well-being experienced, like the gathering of clouds, is the appearance of a new lease of life, called samudaya. The gradual dwindling away of vigour after five or six hours, when the nutriment has been consumed, is called nirodha. So the Buddha said, "When nutrition arises, materiality arises; when nutrition ceases, materiality ceases."

The Practice Leading to the Cessation of Materiality

The knowledge that has perceived the first, second, and third aspects of materiality is called mundane right view, which develops into supramundane right view or path knowledge after application.

Right thought, the indispensable associate of right view, is also of two types: mundane right thought and right thought as path knowledge. In our example above, the visualization of the process of change in the flame is the function of right view. What brings forth this visualization is right thought. Only when right thought prevails can right view occur. The meditator's insight into the incessant arising and vanishing of materiality is due to the presence of right view. Bringing right view into focus is the function of right thought.

How Does Right Thought Function?

It focuses one's attention on the unsatisfactoriness of life. The immensity of the need for food in all living things, the need for a regular food intake, not less than twice a day; how one feels when one is full, when one begins to feel hungry, and when one starves. It lets one imagine the hypothetical consequences of a great famine in this continent of Asia—how soon this whole continent would be turned into a vast graveyard. These kinds of reflections are called right thought.

If one contemplates the constant changes taking place in one's body, even during a single sitting one may discern the arising and vanishing of physical phenomena. At the start of a sitting, nothing in particular is felt, for the body is at ease. After a while, slight heat is often felt either in the legs or another part of the body, then you may feel the heat intensify; then you might feel numb; then a tingling sensation, then discomfort in the legs, etc. Such changes, which are bound to occur, can readily be observed.

By closely observing the phenomena within oneself, the continuous arising of new materiality is perceived, like the gathering of clouds. Then at once, the disappearance of those same phenomena is perceived, like clouds being wafted away by the wind. This is the function of right view. The focusing of attention on directly observable phenomena is the function of right thought. It is only with the appropriate application of right thought that right view can clearly discern the true nature of phenomena. In fact, such perception can occur in any posture for, whether you notice it or not, phenomena arise and vanish all the time.

Once right view and right thought are established as supramundane insight, three factors mature that can remove all bodily and verbal misconduct, for which the latent tendency has accumulated. These three factors are right speech, right action, and right livelihood. Then, right effort means zeal in one's undertaking. It also goes by the name "*ātappa*," which means "that which harasses the defilements." Another name for right effort is *sammappadhāna*. It has three aspects: *ārambha*, *nikkama*, and *parakkama*. *Ārambha* is promptitude and exertion. *Nikkama* is alertness that does not tolerate sloth, torpor, and indolence. *Parakkama* is vigour that never allows one to slacken in one's right efforts. It is due to the lack of this kind of effort that people do not attain to jhāna and path knowledge.

Right mindfulness means the constant awareness that does not allow the mind to stray from the object of contemplation even for a fraction of a second.

Right concentration is steadiness of the mind that does not slip off its object of contemplation.

These latter six constituents of the path are also each of two types, mundane and supramundane. Here, we are concerned only with the supramundane factors.

These eight factors are the Truth of the Path. Of these eight, right speech, right action, and right livelihood appear automatically once a meditator has achieved insight. The aim of insight meditation is to perceive the real nature of one's body in the ultimate sense, which dispels delusion. To develop insight, one needs right mindfulness, right effort, right concentration, and right thought. With these four factors as the locomotive, right view is ready for the inward journey. The right track for the journey is just a fathom in length: the height of an average human. This journey is the close observation of phenomena taking place within one's body, from head to foot. Then, concept will gradually yield to perception. By doggedly pursuing this perception, one can, with sufficient diligence, knock at the door of nibbāna in seven days' time. If not in seven days, it might take one month, or one year, or two, three, or up to seven years. This is explicitly mentioned at various places in the texts. Remember nirodha in its second meaning, i.e. the total cessation of the five aggregates and rebirth is nirodha, which is nibbāna. This is the supramundane nirodha.

The Satisfaction in Materiality

"The pleasure and joy arising dependent on materiality constitute the satisfaction *(assāda)* in materiality."

In the fifth aspect requiring proficiency in materiality, by the term *"assāda"* the text means the pleasure one can enjoy in the favourable planes of existence: wealthy human existence, the six celestial realms, or the brahmā realms. It means the physical well-being, pleasure, and joy that can be experienced in those existences. Here, we shall confine the explanation to human existence.

When a pleasing visual object, such as a beautiful shape or colour, contacts the eye, seeing occurs and a pleasant feeling coupled with joy arises. Just as ants are very fond of honey or treacle, sentient beings are very fond of pleasure and joy. Just as moths are captivated by the light of a flame, beings are captivated by pleasure and joy. This is the pleasant aspect of materiality, i.e. the delight in the eye and a visual object.

In the same way, when a melodious sound contacts the ear, hearing occurs, and a pleasant feeling coupled with joy arises. When a delicious taste contacts the tongue, tasting occurs, and a pleasant feeling coupled with joy arises. When something agreeable to the touch contacts the body, every part of which is sensitive to touch, touching occurs, and a pleasant feeling coupled with joy arises.

The mind may be likened to the crystal-clear water that gushes up from a spring, for it manifests from the heart-base in pristine purity. It can take any of the six sense objects as its object. So when an agreeable sense object or mental object comes into its range, either apprehension or comprehension occurs, and a pleasant feeling coupled with joy arises. However, since we are currently discussing the aggregate of materiality, the mind will not be dealt with here.

The Danger in Materiality

"The transience, unsatisfactoriness, and instability of materiality constitute the danger *(ādīnava)* in materiality."

In the sixth aspect requiring proficiency in materiality, the transient nature of materiality will be evident if one perceives the burden of seeking nutrition, the arising and cessation taking place in one's body, as in the analogy of the man-sized flame. The daily struggle to earn a living, the constant care the body needs, the arduous acquisition of wealth, are burdensome, and these activities take place due to this body. When this truth is perceived by insight knowledge, that is right view.

Liability to disease and death, to all sorts of hazards such as fire, drowning, venomous snakes, wild beasts, evil spirits, or accidents that might cause injury or death, are all manifestations of the changeable nature of materiality. They are obvious to one with right view. This is the sixth aspect.

I shall now illustrate the fifth and sixth aspects. The British administrative authorities, in their campaign to get rid of stray dogs, used poisoned meat, which was thrown about wherever there were stray dogs. The dogs, being enticed by the flavour and rich taste of the bait, rushed for it, little suspecting any danger. The result is obvious. Herein, the enticing flavour and rich taste are the satisfaction in the poisoned meat, the hidden poison in the meat is its danger. This is an illustration of how pleasure lures the unwary and how danger besets them. Here the real culprits are the four external enemies: the colour, the smell, the taste, and the poison in the meat, and the four internal enemies: the eye, the nose, the tongue, and craving. Poison alone would not have caused the death of the dogs unless it was hidden in the meat. Poison hidden inside a lump of clay would be no danger because it lacks the attraction. If the dogs had no eye, no nose, no tongue, and no craving the attractive poison could not have endangered them either. It is only because the external and the internal agencies worked together that the dogs succumbed to them.

Let's take another example, the example of the baited hook in fishing. You should understand on proper reflection that the materiality constituting yourself, your family, and all material objects such as food, shelter, and clothing, are in reality like baited hooks. The pleasure and joy arising from craving for all these things are just like the attractions of the bait. It is because you have lustfully snatched them and taken them to be your own property that you are subjected to the poisonous influence of those possessions, being harassed daily. In fact, those possessions are impermanent, unsatisfactory, and unstable materiality, fraught with evil consequences.

Q. How does impermanence oppress you every day? How does unsatisfactoriness oppress you every day? How does instability oppress you every day?

A. Impermanence is the accomplice of death. It is an ogre or a forest fire that devours everything. It consumes one's food from one's mother's milk until the last drop of water on one's deathbed. It also consumes the fresh cells and all forms of materiality, namely kamma-originated materiality and consciousness-originated materiality that are sustained by regular feeding. The ogre of impermanence devours everything taken into our body, leaving nothing. It is just like feeding a huge flame with oil. Try to perceive how, for instance, the nutrition that sustains the eye is fully consumed by the ogre that works in the eye. Likewise try to perceive this with respect to the other organs.

To give a further example: A certain man has a spendthrift wife. He works hard and hands over all his earnings to her while she stays at home squandering it. Give her a hundred, she makes short shrift of it; give her a thousand, ten thousand, any amount—her desire for spending is never satiated. Just imagine how a man would feel with such a wife who enslaves him and causes his ruin. Likewise, the ogre of impermanence that lurks within us oppresses us everywhere. Unsatisfactoriness also oppresses us in the same way. The way that instability oppresses us is only too evident.

The Escape from Materiality

"The abandonment of desire and lust for materiality constitutes the escape *(nissaraṇa)* from materiality."

In the seventh aspect requiring proficiency in materiality, the Buddha points to the escape, right now, from the clutches of materiality. When right view arises in one who perceives the pleasures and dangers of materiality, that is the escape from materiality. Those twin accomplices have been oppressing us incessantly throughout the infinite cycle of rebirth.

The truth of the origin of suffering is craving, which is manifested in desire and attachment to the body. How do desire and attachment cling to one's body? One believes, "This is my body; this is my hand, my leg, my head, my eye, and so on." Furthermore, when the eye sees something, one believes, "I see it." Likewise one believes, "I hear it," "I smell it," "I taste it," or "I touch it." The cessation of craving, which is the origin of all suffering, is the escape from materiality.

It is only when craving is present that new aggregates of materiality arise after one's death. If craving is extinguished right now, no fresh materiality will arise after death. This will then be the last death, for there is no materiality or no "body" to suffer another death. That is how one escapes from materiality. This should now be quite clear.

Seven Aspects of Feeling to be Perceived

The remaining aggregates will be explained only in brief.

The True Nature of Feeling

"O bhikkhus, there are six kinds of feeling: feeling originating in eye-contact, feeling originating in ear-contact, feeling originating in nose-contact, feeling originating in tongue-contact, feeling originating in body-contact, feeling originating in mind-contact. When, on seeing a visible object, one feels sad, neutral, or joyous, this is called feeling originating in eye-contact. Similarly, on hearing a sound ... smelling an odour ... savouring a taste ... touching some tangible object ... thinking some thought, when the contact is felt in the mind and one feels sad, neutral, or joyous, that feeling is called feeling originating in mind-contact."

If something causes a pleasant feeling, you call it "good"; if it causes an unpleasant feeling, you call it "bad." These are the criteria by which the world judges things, animate or inanimate, and you value those things accordingly. So we set a value on visible objects depending on how much pleasure they give to the eye. The greater the pleasure, the higher the value. Similarly with the other sense objects. Remember the great fondness of ants for honey or treacle that we illustrated in our discussion on the aggregate of materiality.

The Origin and Cessation of Feeling

When some visible object, such as a shape or colour, contacts the eye, a continuous stream of feelings caused by the contact arises. These feelings are called "feelings originating in eye-contact." When the visible object disappears, the feelings cease immediately. The arising of the feelings in the eye is called the origin of the feeling originating in eye-contact. The ceasing of those feelings is called the cessation of the feeling originating in eye-contact. If you want to experience the feeling again, you have to look at the object again. The moment the contact between the object and eye is re-established, the feelings in the eye arise again. The moment the eye ceases to focus on the object, those feelings cease.

Likewise, when some sound is produced and contacts the ear, a continuous stream of feelings arises in the ear, called "feelings originating in ear-contact." When the sound disappears, those feelings cease at once. If the feeling is to arise again, the sound must be repeated.

The same with a smell: when it is produced and contacts the nose, "feelings originating in nose-contact" arise in the nose. When the smell disappears, the feelings cease.

Again, if sweet or sour food is placed on the tongue, "feelings originating in tongue-contact" arise at the tongue. The moment those tastes disappear, the feelings cease.

When hard or soft, hot or cold, stiff or flaccid objects contact the body, whether internally or externally, "feelings originating in body-contact" arise, wherever the contact is made. When the contact disappears, the feeling ceases totally. When some idea arises in the mind, "feelings originating in mind-contact" arise. When the mind stops thinking of the idea, the feelings cease at once.

The above six kinds of feeling are always being experienced at their respective sense bases. However, those lacking in right view take them not just as feelings, but as "I see it," "I hear it," etc. This is the tenacious, mistaken view called "personality view" or "ego-belief" *(sakkāyadiṭṭhi)*. When pleasant feelings arise, the average deluded person thinks, "I feel fine." When unpleasant feelings arise, they think, "I feel depressed." Thus the ego is always assumed to exist with respect to all feelings that arise and vanish at the six sense bases.

Just as the microbes infesting a sore can only be observed through a microscope, so only through insight knowledge can one observe the six kinds of feeling rapidly arising and vanishing at their respective sense bases. All the six kinds of feelings arise due to contact.

From Contact Arises Feeling

When a sense object meets its corresponding sense base, the mind adverts to the external sense object. That is what is meant by contact. Only when the mind adverts well does apprehension arise, and only when the sense object is apprehended does feeling arises. Since the feeling arises only from contact, it is called "feeling originating in contact." It is like saying "Jack, son of Richard" for clearer identification. Since feeling has contact as its origin, when contact disappears, feeling ceases.

The Practice Leading to the Cessation of Feeling

What has been said about the fourth aspect concerning materiality applies here too. Herein, right view means insight into the aggregate of feeling. It also means penetrating knowledge of the aggregate of materiality.

The Satisfaction and Danger in Feeling

It was said above that the pleasant feeling, which causes pleasure and joy, is the satisfaction in materiality. With materiality, feeling is the agency that brings pleasure and joy. With feeling itself, now as both the principal and the agent, the satisfaction has double significance. Hence, the danger that lurks in feeling is also far greater than with materiality, as it has a more immediate effect.

The feeling of enjoyment of an object occurs at its relevant sense base only while the object and the sense base are in contact. With the disappearance of the object at its relevant door, the feeling vanishes instantly. So we feel a pleasant taste only while it is on the tongue or palate, and the moment we swallow it, the feeling is no more. In fact, the feeling is lost even at the upper end of the tongue itself. This transience is observable in the feelings connected with all six senses. Therefore, contemplate hard to perceive the constant oppression of feeling caused by its transience, instability, and unsatisfactoriness.

The Escape from Feeling

The means of escape is within you. The feelings that arise in you can never be dangerous if you are not captivated by them. When the craving for feeling ceases, the danger is simply not there at all. To one who does not care for gold or silver, the dangers associated with them do not arise. In other words, a penniless man need have no fear of thieves. It is only if one is highly pleased with one's property, that the dangers to that property cause worry. If one does not cling to the property but is quite detached from it, the property is not dangerous. Detachment from the feelings as they arise is the escape from feeling.

Seven Aspects of Perception to be Perceived

The text for the aggregate of perception does not differ much from that for the aggregate of feeling, in most places; one has only to substitute the word *saññā* for *vedanā*. In the definition it goes as: perception of a visual object, perception of sound, perception of smell, perception of taste, perception of touch, and perception of ideas.

From early infancy, one has learnt to recognize and memorize things. Beginning from "That's Mum," "That's Dad," "That's Teddy," to all the things that a child takes notice of—the time of day, the directions, etc.—the process of noting and remembering things with their names is what is meant by perception. Perceptions, of course, go with the six sense objects. A visual object can only be recognized and memorized by the eye, a sound only by the ear, and so on. Perception then widens to abstract ideas, skills, knowledge, beliefs, etc., according to one's upbringing, race, tradition, culture, and the plane of one's existence. The first five kinds of perception should need no further explanation.

Dhammasaññā is the conception that perceives the eye, the ear, the nose, the tongue, the body (as the sense base), the mind (i.e. concepts of good or bad, etc.); the sensations or feelings, concepts or perceptions, volitions or will, applied thought, sustained thought, effort, desire; greed, anger, pride, or conceit; confidence, wisdom; killing as misconduct, stealing as misconduct, lying as misconduct; giving as meritorious deed, virtue as meritorious deed, wisdom or attainment of proficiency in insight training; and so forth. These, and a myriad other perceptions, are recognized and remembered. They are not taught, but learnt from one's natural environment and imbued by culture and tradition. One born in a virtuous family is likely to acquire perceptions about virtuous things. One born in the family of a hunter or fisherman is likely to acquire perceptions about wicked things. Thus perceptions can have an infinite range. Contemplate diligently to gain insight into perception as a separate element within yourself and in others.

When a person says, "I remember" or "I know," these are usually just instances of a deluded belief in the existence of a person or a self when, in fact, there is no such thing. The truth is that there are only phenomena, which arise and vanish due to relevant conditions. For example, a leper can never see the carrier germs infecting the sores on his body. With the aid of a microscope a doctor can let him see the germs, ever arising and decaying. Then he should realize, perhaps to his consternation, that the sores are not his, but the habitat of the germs only. Similarly, when you gain insight, you can see empirically that there is no self but just perceptions originating at the six sense bases. Only then do you perceive rightly, which is insight knowledge. What you have all along recognized and remembered as "my eye" is merely the material quality of sense cognition. What you thought was "I see" is just feeling originating in eye-contact. What you thought was "my seeing" is but the perception of form or colour. Try to realize the truth of the other perceptions likewise. Then you will see that it is just a play of the six perceptions on your mind, which is deluded by your own ignorant bias into thinking and believing firmly that they are your acts of knowing and remembering.

The remaining six aspects in the aggregate of perception will be discussed later in the discussion on the aggregate of consciousness.

Seven Aspects of Mental Formations to be Perceived

Rūpasañcetanā means the volition behind the function of seeing visual forms. So for the six mental formations associated with the six sense objects we have six volitions. The Buddha mentions volition in this context because it is the leading factor, though there are many other mental formations such as: contact *(phassa)*, one-pointedness *(ekaggatā)*, attention *(manasikāra)*, initial application *(vitakka)*, sustained application *(vicāra)*, energy *(viriya)*, joy *(pīti)*, will *(chanda)*, greed *(lobha)*, hatred *(dosa)*, delusion *(moha)*, wrong view *(diṭṭhi)*, pride *(māna)*, envy *(issā)*, meanness *(macchariya)*, worry *(kukkucca)*, sloth *(thina)*, torpor *(middha)*, doubt *(vicikicchā)*, confidence *(saddhā)*, mindfulness *(sati)*, moral shame *(hirī)*, moral dread *(ottappa)*, and wisdom *(paññā)*.

The Analogy of the Train

In a locomotive, the steam motivates the engine whose constituent parts function together and drive the locomotive. The engine starts functioning due to steam-power and it goes on working due to the presence of steam-power. All the parts of the engine are motivated simultaneously so that they work in harmony, with the capacity to pull the train at a good speed for long distances.

This body is like the train. The heart-base is like the boiler of the engine. Volition is like the steam-power, which motivates the moving parts of the engine. As volition arises, it motivates the various parts of the body through the material quality that is the element of motion. This motivating power is astonishingly powerful; it acts very rapidly, and motivates all the limbs in the required manner of movement. It is just like the train being pulled along the track by steam-power. This is how volition drives bodily actions.

The volition working behind speech may be compared to the whistle that the boiler occasionally produces. The volition working in the mind may be likened to the steam generated by the boiler.

Volition associated with greed directs its motivating force onto the bodily, verbal, and mental functioning of the body so that actions arise, which manifest greed. In the same way, volition associated with hatred or anger motivates the functioning of the body, so that bodily and verbal expressions and a mental attitude of anger are the result. Other volitions, such as initial application, sustained application, or energy, also motivate the bodily, verbal, and mental functions. They result in applying the mind to an object *(vitakka)*, or fixing the mind onto an object *(vicāra)*, or putting effort into a task *(viriya)*. Similarly, it should be understood that all wholesome or unwholesome deeds, speech, and thoughts have the corresponding volitions activating them. For instance, an act of faith is motivated by saddhā; when one is mindful, sati is the underlying force, and so on.

Those who do not understand the element of volition have conceit due to personality view. Self-view is firmly entrenched in them. All their bodily movements are taken as their own actions: "I sit," "I stand," "I speak," "I do this," etc. All mental activities are taken as their own: "I think," "I have an idea," "I remember," "I know," etc. The truth is that all our activities are just expressions of their underlying volitions. Each is actuated by an appropriate volition like the steam-power that motivates the locomotive. That is why, in the aggregate of mental formations, the element of volition is singled out by the Buddha from the other mental concomitants.

Some Examples of how Attachment to Personality View Works

"I touch it" is a delusion about *phassa*.

"I feel happy," "I feel miserable," "I am delighted," "I feel sorry" are delusions about *vedanā*.

"I know," "I remember" are delusions about *saññā*.

"I have concentration" is delusion about *ekaggatā*.

"I am paying attention to it" is delusion about *manasikāra*.

"I apply my mind to such and such" is delusion about *vitakka*.

"I keep my mind steadfastly on it" is delusion about *vicāra*.

"I make an effort" is delusion about *viriya*.

"I feel joyful" is delusion about *pīti*.

"I want to do this, to see this, to hear this, to go there, to come, to say, to know, to get, to take" are delusions about *chanda*.

"I love her," "I like him," "I adore them," "I want it," "I am very fond of that" are delusions about *lobha*.

"I hate it," "I can't bear that person," "I am angry," "I resent it," "I am disappointed" are delusions about *dosa*.

"I do not understand," "I am confused" are delusions about *moha*.

"I hold the wrong view" is delusion about *diṭṭhi*.

"I won't give in," "I wish to excel," "I am superior to him," "I am equal to him" are delusions about *māna*.

"I envy him" is delusion about *issā*.

"I don't want to share this" is delusion about *macchariya*.

"I feel lazy" is delusion about *thīna-middha*.

"I can't decide" is delusion about *vicikicchā*.

"I revere him," "I believe its truth" are delusions about *saddhā*.

"I am not being forgetful" is delusion about *sati.*

"I understand" is delusion about *paññā.*

"I am ashamed to do evil," "I dread it" are delusions about *hirī* and *ottappa.*

"I kill" is delusion about self-view in the volition of killing.

"I steal" is delusion about self-view in the volition of stealing.

"I make an offering," "I give a gift" are delusions about the volition behind giving charity.

All those deeds, words, and thoughts are egocentric. Apparently good or bad, the delusion of a self in them renders them all unwholesome. They are the underwriters for a passage to hell. They are stumbling blocks to insight. They are detrimental to the realization of nibbāna. They belong to this side of the ocean of rebirths. Release from those beliefs means nibbāna, the yonder shore of saṃsāra. Attachment to the deluded "I" in all actions is what draws you into the floods of saṃsāra. Abandonment of attachment to personality view means to cross the great ocean of saṃsāra.

This is just a random list of ways in which personality view, the darkest type of wrong view, deludes the average person.

Since volition is the key factor behind any action, if one can discard attachment to the nonexistent self in respect of volition, personality view becomes extinct. If personality view in volition can be eradicated from one's psyche, the other mental factors can never again be associated with the deluded self. That is why the Buddha highlighted volition in describing the aggregate of mental formations. The remaining mental formations should be understood in the same way.

Seven Aspects of Consciousness to be Perceived

The True Nature of Consciousness

When someone wishes to see the moon, he focuses his eyes on the moon. The moon's image is then reflected onto a sensitive material quality, which is the eye-base. The same principle holds in respect of other clear, smooth surfaces like glass or water where the image of the moon is reflected. The occurrence of the reflection at the eye-base has a terrific impact comparable to a bolt of lightning. This impact on the sensitivity of the eye arouses an instantaneous succession of units of consciousness at the eye-base called "eye-consciousness." When the viewer turns away from the moon, the image disappears, and with it the eye-consciousness also disappears. Then the viewer says he does not see the moon. What is called "seeing" is, in truth, just the eye-consciousness. "Not seeing" is just the disappearance of this eye-consciousness. Although images are reflected onto clear, smooth surfaces like glass or water, no consciousness arises because the materiality there is of the type originating in physical change. It is merely a base that can receive the image called an "appearance-base."

When you look into a mirror, your face appears in the mirror; when you turn away, the image is no longer there. You simply say you saw it there, and now you don't see it there. However, you are unlikely to realize that it is only eye-consciousness arising and vanishing. This is the exposition of eye-consciousness.

By the same principle, when a sound contacts the ear-base, a tremendous impact like a clap of thunder is felt on the sensitive ear-base. At that instant, a rapid succession of units of ear-consciousness arises at the ear-base. The moment the sound disappears, consciousness ceases. You would simply say that you heard it, and now you don't hear it, but the truth about the phenomenon of ear-consciousness is rarely realized.

When a smell contacts the nose, the sensitive base for smell, nose-consciousness arises incessantly. When the smell disappears, the consciousness also instantly disappears. People say, "I smelled it," "I cannot smell it now." Little do they realize that it is only the phenomenon of nose-consciousness.

When some tasty morsel is placed on the tongue, tongue-consciousness arises at the tongue-base. When the object of taste leaves the tongue-base, the consciousness disappears. "I tasted it," "I don't taste it now," people would say, oblivious of the arising and vanishing of tongue-consciousness.

When the element of extension, heat, or motion contacts the body, tactile-consciousness arises at the point. When the external object disappears, tactile-consciousness disappears. If some cold water or a cool breeze touches one's back, the whole back becomes the sense base and tactile-consciousness arises there. We then say, "My back feels cold." When the water or breeze disappears, the consciousness ceases, and we say there is no cold feeling there. We do not realize that it is the arising and cessation of tactile-consciousness. When we stay in the sun we feel hot and stuffy throughout our body, but we rarely recognize it as the arising of tactile-consciousness. Bodily feelings are also felt from time to time in the head, chest, stomach, and so on. We know it aches when there is a sensation of stiffness; we know it tingles when a limb is numb, we know it is painful, hot, tired, and so on. However, more likely than not, we do not recognize those feelings as the arising of tactile-consciousness. Remember here, too, the analogy of using a microscope to examine a leprous sore.

There is an ever-present process called "the element of apprehension" *(manodhātu)* depending on the heart-base, which is so pure as to be lustrous. The mind-base is a functional state of subconsciousness *(bhavaṅga)*. When a visible object contacts the eye, the impact is simultaneously felt at the mind-base. So when one is looking at the moon, the image of the moon appears at both the eye-base and the mind-base simultaneously. When the viewer turns away from the moon, the image on the eye disappears instantly, but the image on the mind-base disappears rather slowly. So too, when sounds appear at the ear-base, they simultaneously make an impact on the mind-base too. Similarly, smells, tastes and tactile-objects, while impacting on their respective sense bases, also make impressions on the mind.

Imagine a piece of glass the shape and size of a man. Imagine a crystal ball, set inside the human-shaped glass block. All sorts of external objects—houses and trees, mountains and woods, men and animals, the sun, the moon, and the stars—will be reflected onto the glass block and the crystal ball inside simultaneously. You could see, for instance, the image of the sun on the glass block and also on the crystal ball. This simile is to help you visualize the phenomenon of the mind-base.

The above is the detailed explanation of how the five sense objects appear at the respective sense bases, while making their impressions on the mind-base simultaneously.

Apart from those five sense objects entering through the five sense bases, the mind-base can also generate an infinite variety of mental objects just by application of thought. These objects are purely mental. Whereas the five sense objects must present themselves at their respective sense doors to make their impressions, the mind-objects need not actually exist. Whatever has been seen, heard, felt, or experienced can make its impression on the mind at the mind-base. The mind-base has an infinite range of capacities differing from one being to another. So the mind-bases of a Buddha, a Solitary Buddha, a Chief Disciple, a Senior Disciple, or an Ordinary Disciple vary widely in their range. So too, for beings born with three wholesome roots, with two wholesome roots, or without wholesome roots; human beings, earthbound devas, *catumahārāja devas*, the *Tāvatiṃsa devas*, the higher devas and the *brahmās;* the purity and capacities vary enormously between each abode.

The mind-base of the Buddha is incomparably pure and radiant. It can be conscious of anything in the infinite universe, an infinite range of kammic forces, an infinite number of beings, or an infinite range of conditioned phenomena. The sublime Dhamma of the Four Noble Truths can arise as a mental object only in those born with three wholesome roots, which implies a certain maturity by way of perfections.

The Origin and Cessation of the Four Mental Aggregates

I shall now give a brief exposition on the four mental aggregates: feeling, perception, mental formations, and consciousness.

The Buddha declared that the first three of those aggregates originate from contact. The aggregate of consciousness originates from psychophysical phenomena. The significance of this will be explained here. Although the aggregate of consciousness is mentioned last in the Buddha's exposition on the five aggregates, in many ways it is the most important of the four mental aggregates. The Buddha said:

"All mental states have mind as their forerunner. Mind is their chief and they are mind-made."

Again, he said:

"Mind is the lord of the six sense doors."

So consciousness is the premier among the four, or in other words, it is the leader of the other three, the lord of those three. When we say a sense object appears on the sense base, this appearance is caused by consciousness only.

Let us give an analogy here. Suppose there is a sense object in the form of a juice-bearing root. The root is first received by consciousness. Contact crushes it and strains it. When the juice is produced and strained, feeling savours it, feeling pleasant or unpleasant, and perception notes how it tastes—sweet or sour. Then, on getting that information, volition starts motivating the respective organs of the body to function. It expresses itself in bodily and verbal action and in framing the mind, thus leading to mental formation's part in the mental process.

So contact is the key factor for feeling, perception, and mental formations. However, it is not the key factor for consciousness, which is the leader of them all. Yet consciousness cannot function without feeling, perception, and mental formations. That is why the Buddha says that the arising and cessation of consciousness is dependent on mental properties. If consciousness is likened to a flame, then feeling, perception, and mental formations are like the light of the flame. When the flame goes out, the three die a natural death, instantly. If the flame arises again, the three reappear together. If the arising and cessation of consciousness can be understood, the arising and cessation of the trio can readily be understood. Hence the arising and cessation of consciousness will be explained further.

The Origin and Cessation of Subconsciousness

When a person is asleep, the mind is in a state of subcons-ciousness *(bhavaṅga)*. This very subtle state of mind is always present in a living being, hovering around the heart-base like clear water oozing from a spring. It is an inert state of mind below the threshold of consciousness. So it cannot motivate the sense organs to function, either in bodily, verbal, or mental action. It cannot advert to mental objects. The heart-base is an offshoot of the four primary elements. Its vitality and health depend totally on the vitality and health of materiality, because the four primary elements are themselves dependent on the nutriment of the body.

Subconsciousness persists as long as the heart-base lasts. When the heart-base ceases, subconsciousness also ceases.

For example, a rainbow is seen due to the presence of rain clouds. Once the rain clouds are wafted away by the wind, the rainbow cannot remain. To give another example, a powerful deva, by his magical power, creates a string of highly combustible material as he runs along, letting the string burn as he runs. The fireworks would last only as long as the combustible string lasts, no longer.

If you reckon how long it lasts, say, for an hour, in that time trillions of material phenomena would have perished. Just as the deva's string is made to appear afresh along with him, while fresh materiality continues to arise in the heart-base, subconsciousness also arises from it. Just as the string is consumed by the fire, so also the heart-base is decaying all the time and with it the subconsciousness too is decaying. The arising of fresh subconsciousness is called the arising of consciousness. Its cessation is called the cessation of consciousness.

The arising and vanishing of subconsciousness can be perceived when contemplation is exercised along with the materiality of the heart-base. It is too subtle to discern by consciousness alone. Lacking practical means of observing it, one is apt to rationalize, referring to this or that text, but rationalizing is not conducive to insight knowledge. It is not called training in insight at all.

The Origin and Cessation of Consciousness

I shall now explain how the process of consciousness arises in the six sense bases.

When we look at the moon, the image of the moon appears simultaneously at the eye-base and the heart-base. The sense object, which is the image of the moon, rudely invades the eye-base with terrific force. It is like the sparking when the steel hammer strikes the flint in a lighter. The image of the moon makes its impact there, like a bolt of lightning. Eye-consciousness arises in the eye at that instant. Similarly, the terrific impression of the image of the moon appears at the heart-base, and mind-consciousness is stirred up with dazzling intensity. It is not unlike the lightning that flashes in rain clouds. When consciousness arises, subconsciousness disappears. Eye-consciousness taking place at the eye-base, and the flashes of mind-consciousness reacting to the contact at the heart-base, thereby complete the function of receiving the impression of the moon. This goes on for as long as the contact between the eye and the moon lasts. When the viewer turns away, all those units of consciousness disappear. The ignorant person thinks that he or she sees the moon. However, it is only the occurrence of flashes of consciousness in the eye and the mind that take place. Personality view clings to a delusive "I" based on the occurrence of consciousness.

Just as darkness reasserts itself when a flash of lighting disappears, consciousness ceases and subconsciousness reasserts itself at the heart-base the moment the moon gets out of the eye. The "not seeing" is noticed by the average deluded person who thinks, "I don't see the moon now." Personality view makes him or her think so, of course. For had there been a "person" who had seen the moon earlier, that person should have died along with the cessation of "seeing." This is the delusion dominating an ignorant person.

The Noble Ones, being possessed of right view, see the truth as it is. As contact occurs between the eye and the moon, transient moments of consciousness occur that cognize the material object called the moon. This transient consciousness occurs with dazzling flashes inside the body, like flashes of lightning. These conscious moments are as fleeting as flashes of lightning in their disappearance too. This is how the undeluded ones see it.

In the example of lightning, clouds are not lightning, nor is lightning the clouds. Cloud is cloud, and lightning is lightning. With a clashing of clouds, lightning occurs for just that fleeting moment. The lightning thus produced does not go back into the clouds. Nor does it go anywhere. It simply disappears. Try to extend this analogy to understand consciousness of all the six kinds.

> "Like the occurrence of lightning in the sky, all things, whether mind or matter, occur in flashes as conditions arise for such occurrence. Quick as lightning, they are gone."
>
> (*Visuddhimagga*)

During a momentary blinking of the eye, seeing is momentarily interrupted. This is a practical example showing the discontinuity of eye-consciousness. Seeing and not seeing are quite evident. Just remember the analogy: lightning is lightning, cloud is cloud. Regard consciousness as similar to the phenomenon of lightning. Try to understand the instant of its arising, and the instant of its cessation.

By day, visible objects are everywhere within the awareness of the eye-base, so we are easily deluded into thinking that we see them continuously. However, if you are attentive, you can probably recognize the cessation of consciousness in seeing one object as your attention is turned to another. The same process of sense cognition takes place at the ear-base, the nose-base, the tongue-base, and the body-base too.

While various sounds come within the range of the ear, their impact is felt at the ear-base and the heart-base. There, flashes of consciousness arise, only to stop altogether the moment the sound vanishes. Then the transient flashes of consciousness vanish and die. This process of arising and cessation constitutes ear-consciousness.

Except during sleep, sense contacts are always occurring at the five sense bases. None of them makes its impression concurrently with another. At any given moment, the dominant sense prevails to arouse consciousness. Not one remains even for a moment—each one that has arisen ceases instantly. This characteristic of consciousness will become clear if you contemplate properly.

The Origin and Cessation of Mind-Consciousness

The subject of volitional mind-consciousness is very profound. The flashes of consciousness are highly transient, and arise independent of the five sense organs. Here, only the basics will be explained. When aroused by external sense objects through the five sense doors, consciousness flashes onto the mind, which merely takes cognizance of it. Those flashes of consciousness function like flashes of lightning that let one momentarily see the lay of the land in the dark. So too with the sense-consciousness that arises from contact between sense objects and the sense bases. They are merely recognized as such and such, that is all. By themselves, they cannot activate the body, but merely let the mind know that a certain thing is of this shape or colour, or this kind of sound, smell, taste, or touch, and so on.

It is only mind-consciousness, arising at the heart-base, that can motivate the bodily organs and the mind itself, with the tremendous force of a storm or a clap of thunder. It activates the parts of the body to produce bodily actions, speech, or the appropriate frame of mind. Then the mind can dwell on a myriad of mind-objects in the abstract. This is generally called "thinking."

Volition is the power that causes every action like the steam in a locomotive, steamer, or electricity-generating station. The heart-base is the power-station from where arteries and veins branch out over the whole body. Just as a power-station transmits electricity throughout the country along a network of cables, the heart-base generates material qualities of motion in the body whenever the impulsion arises. The organs respond to the impulse immediately. Whenever a fingertip or a small toe is hurt, the heart-base "knows" it at once.

These similes are just aids to visualizing the complex psychophysical process. The underlying principle is the main point. If one sees materiality, but the principle of elements occurring from conditions is missed, one is apt to cling to a delusive personality view, which will then predominate.

You should reject personality view in the light of the truth. Do not let yourself be deluded by the wrong view that there is such a thing as a person, and that "I" exist; that such and such are my concerns, such are my doings, etc. See the fact of psychophysical phenomena in everything within and around you. Try to visualize the interplay of psychophysical phenomena whenever any action takes place in you, from the slightest blinking to explosions of fury (if this ever happens!). If you are vigilant, you can perceive the amazing events that are just the incessant, conditioned occurrence of phenomena, quite independently of you or your wishes.

Apparently, this body seems quite solid, substantial, and unchanging. Its instability escapes our attention. We are apt to think a thing is not changing under two circumstances: when change is so rapid that we cannot normally notice it, or when the thing does not change by its very nature. When you look at the blackness of space, you never think it undergoes any change at all, because it is not a changeable phenomenon.

All psychophysical phenomena change billions of times within a blink of the eyes. Yet we barely notice that whole period of one blink, for it seems so rapid to us. This body changes at a staggering rate beyond normal comprehension. This rapidity creates the illusion of continuity, an inborn notion strengthened by nature. If sustained right thinking can be focused on the arising and cessation of phenomena in and around you, you will come to understand the changeable nature of all phenomena.

Let me illustrate. Imagine a water tank the size of a man, filled with water and placed upright. Think about the mass of still water in the tank. Imagine pulling the tank towards you just slightly, say, for half an inch at the top. You will see the water being disturbed and the whole mass of it being inclined towards you. Next, imagine pushing the tank in the opposite direction, when the water will incline away from you. Even if you just shake the tank very lightly or tap it, you would notice that the water is disturbed. There is no solidity, no unchangeable mass of water at all. Apply this illustration to the psychophysical phenomena that make up your body, and understand their changeability.

So, psychophysical phenomena are mere processes; there is no substance at all in them, not the tiniest atom that is solid or stable. That is why they are liable to change like the water in the tank. This illustrates the transient nature of things and the rapidity of change.

Now I will illustrate the rapidity of action or motion. As you rise from bed, your conscious mind impels your whole body to move through the element of motion, which originates in the mind. Once that element arises due to your impulsion, the previous posture of lying, which is temporary, ceases instantly. The sinews and muscles of that lying posture die out there and then.

Try to visualize the change from the lying posture to the newly-arisen sitting posture. The change is too rapid for the undeveloped mind to comprehend—not to speak of seeing it with the eye. It is only through insight that it can be comprehended. Even with insight you cannot catch up with the rapidity of the change of phenomena, not even one thousandth of its speed. The ordinary human faculties are only rapid enough to enable us to move about through the functioning of the element of motion, which controls bodily movement. They cannot enable us to fly.

The volition of one possessed of supernormal powers is so rapid as to master the forces of the element of motion that can keep the body in the air. One who has attained to uplifting joy *(ubbegā pīti)* can also float in the air like a piece of fluff or a cloud. In both cases, volition has attained supernormal dimensions. By supernormal dimensions is meant the power that can "will" the forces of the element of motion to come into play. Of the four primary elements, only the elements of extension and cohesion have weight. In a human body, these two elements together weigh about fifty or sixty kilos. When impulsion arises through the supernormal faculty or attainment of uplifting joy, the element of motion lifts the whole body so that a state of virtual weightlessness is achieved without effort. The body can float away as lightly as a balloon takes to the air. However, a balloon's flight is very slow compared to jhānic flight. This is mentioned here to show the power of impulsion, the inherent quality of the element of motion, and the rapid change in material phenomena.

> "Through the pervasion of impulsion, which is the element of motion originating in the mind, this body goes, stands or sits."

The element of motion may be compared to the blast of air exploding from the barrel when a gun is fired. It pervades the various organs of the body when volition to execute a certain action impels the mind. The material quality of motion arises at those parts of the body and the desired movements occur. It may also be compared to the steam that rushes out of the boiler in a steam engine, providing the motive power to the pistons and crankshaft.

Impulsion and its Functions

I shall now explain the function of impulsion *(javana)*. The boiler of a locomotive is like the heart-base, the steam-power is like impulsion, but whereas the steam-power pushes once at a stroke, impulsion functions in seven successive moments. Impulsion is a conscious process of tremendous rapidity. Its seven strokes agitate material phenomena in the body like a mine exploding in the water. However, unlike the water being agitated violently, impulsion is under the control of volition, helped by the specific material qualities of expression *(viññatti-rūpa)*. Therefore the movements of the body organs are deliberate, co-ordinated, and orderly. Impulsion occurs billions of times within a blinking of the eyes. There are various kinds of elements of motion involved in any bodily movement. Take walking, for instance. As a man walks, at each step various elements of motion function throughout the body. It is impulsion that gives the necessary impetus to these various elements of motion. It is through its amazing swiftness that such initiation and co-ordination of all bodily functions are effected.

When impulsion sends the message to lift the head, the previous materiality in the head dies out to give way to the new materiality. For example, a firework explodes when ignited. At that instant, the previously cool materiality of the firework is replaced by fiery materiality. The actual process of change from cold to fierce heat starts from the spot where ignition occurs and spreads throughout the firework. When the element of heat undergoes change, all material qualities in association with it change too. So, the elements of extension and motion change, with all other material qualities of colour, smell, taste, and nutritive essence that perish when the cold element perishes. In the ultimate sense, the fiery hot material element and the whole materiality in the firework arise afresh where the cold materiality has ceased.

People say that a person dies when the notion of continuity ceases, i.e. their physical death is observable. In the ultimate sense, however, new psychophysical phenomena arise only after the old phenomena have perished, which is death. This constant perishing of phenomena is also called cessation *(nirodha)* or dissolution *(bhaṅga)*. It is only when one discerns the ultimate truth of this cessation of phenomena that one gains insight. Though one has mastered the seven books of the Abhidhamma Piṭaka, or is a teacher on the ultimate truths for one's whole life, if one has not gained discernment through insight one is just a learned man, not a wise man yet, for one has not empirically understood the

Abhidhamma. Unless one has understood the perishing and cessation of phenomena through direct knowledge, a lifelong habit of teaching about impermanence, unsatisfactoriness, and not-self is futile.

I will now explain the arising and cessation of consciousness flashing around the heart-base and activating the whole body. Here again, the analogy of the train is useful. The incessant puffing of the steam engine, its pushing and its exhaustion, stroke after stroke, is evident on listening to it working. So it is helpful in visualizing the process of the arising and cessation of phenomena. Lightning is another useful example. The heart-base is like the clouds, consciousness is like the flashes of lightning that occur in series of threes, or fours, and then disappear instantly.

The steam engine analogy particularly helps us to visualize the bodily movements, down to the slightest movement of the eyelids, and the activating of consciousness that is constantly arising and ceasing. Not only bodily movement, but verbal and mental activities also come within its scope.

The example of lightning helps us to visualize the sparks of consciousness that clarify cognition at the six sense bases. The intensity of these sparks inside the body, their arising and cessation, are comparable to lightning. The seven strokes of impulsion are inconceivably rapid, so instead of following the text literally, for practical purposes, we can assume that impulsion occurs only once for a blink of the eye. This would be easier to comprehend.

With lightning, both its arising and cessation are evident to the eye. However, the arising and cessation of impulsion, with intervening moments of subconsciousness, is not self-evident. One thinks that the sparks are uninterrupted, because the arising and cessation of consciousness take place so rapidly. Actually, the arising of the impulsions is interrupted by inert moments of subconsciousness when the impulsion ceases. No practical example is available to illustrate this intermittent phenomenon. One has to infer it from the appearance of different mental objects at (supposedly) the same moment. Even while taking a step, various things come to mind. As each new idea enters the mind, the previous object of our attention is dead and gone. Each object is co-existent only with its impulsion. So when we consider the diverse thoughts that our mind wanders to while walking, we can see that the fleeting diversions represent moments of interrupted impulsion. Consider also the process of speaking. With each syllable uttered, there arises (at least) one impulsion that ceases with the uttering of the next syllable. Similarly, with the consciousness at the mind-base, each thought arises only on the cessation of the previous one.

The Origin and Cessation of Feeling, Perception, and Mental Formations

At each step we take, or on seeing or hearing something, pleasure or displeasure arises in us, which is feeling. Each feeling arises and ceases, and a fresh feeling arises and ceases. Then also the perceptions of "this is what is seen," or "that is what is heard," and so on, arise and cease. Then fresh perceptions arise and cease again. What is perceived at the left step vanishes with the advancing of the right step, and so on.

Bodily, verbal, or mental activities are taking place all the time, denoting the arising and cessation of different volitions at each moment:

the arising and cessation of applied thoughts;
the arising and cessation of effort;
the arising and cessation of pleasure and smiles;
the arising and cessation of desire to do something;
the arising and cessation of lust or passion;
the arising and cessation of anger or hatred;
the arising and cessation of conceit;
the arising and cessation of confidence, etc.

Such volitions are always observable. Without right view, however, the observation leads only to false inferences of personality view. With the insight of right view, every observation enhances the knowledge gained already. The arising of those phenomena is called samudaya, and their cessation nirodha.

As for the practice leading to the cessation of these aggregates, what has been said with respect to materiality applies here too.

The Satisfaction and Danger in the Four Mental Aggregates

I shall now explain the satisfaction and danger in the four mental aggregates.

The Satisfaction and Danger in Feeling

In getting what one wants, or in finding what one is looking for, or in experiencing what one longs for, one is pleased. The pleasure and joy derived from such experience is the satisfaction in feeling. The impermanence, the unpleasantness or unsatis-factoriness, and the instability of all four mental aggregates are its danger.

The example of the poisoned meat given to illustrate the satisfaction and danger in materiality is relevant here too. From the viewpoint of the precious opportunity of the Buddhasāsana, the carefree attitude of the multitude who are missing the chance even to escape from the four lower realms is a common instance of the satisfaction and danger in the four mental aggregates. Imprisoned in the filthy confines of sensuality, those ignorant people are constantly oppressed by their own greed, ill-will, and delusion. They have a stubborn attachment to personality view, and have thus booked their passage to the remotest depths of hell.

The dangers of the aggregates of materiality and mentality are both characterized by transience, unsatisfactoriness, and instability, but the transience of mentality is far more rapid. This should be clear from our discussions above on the arising and cessation of these phenomena.

I shall now explain the oppression caused by the transience of feeling. All people have, at some time, been born in the human and celestial realms, and also in the Brahmā realms. There they enjoyed the best of sensual pleasures and the glory of the Brahmā realms. However, being subject to death, which ruthlessly consumes every conditioned existence without leaving any trace, none can ever recollect those previous enjoyments. Such is the transient character of feeling. In the present existence, too, they are forever pursuing sensual pleasures, which cause them only suffering. This yearning for pleasant feeling is only too likely to continue for innumerable rebirths. Thus they are enslaving themselves to the transience of those pleasures. This is how people are forever oppressed by the transient character of feeling.

How, then, does the aggregate of feeling oppress sentient beings with suffering? Herein, suffering has these aspects:

1. Dukkha dukkha—the suffering of physical and mental pain;
2. *Saṅkhāra dukkha*—the suffering of conditioned states;
3. *Vipariṇāma dukkha*—the suffering of changeability or instability.

The first aspect is too obvious to need elucidation.

Whatever pleasant feeling one may be enjoying now is not obtained as a favour from any external power. It is only because one has taken the trouble to acquire merit through giving, virtue, or concentration that pleasant results are enjoyed in this existence. Those meritorious deeds in previous lives have conditioned the present state of well-being. Even when favourable circumstances prevail in the present life, the enjoyment of pleasure still has to be contrived, for pleasure is not built into your system. All too often, pleasurable feeling eludes you even while you are supposed to be having some fun. This is because you can actually feel the pleasant feelings only when they contact your six sense bases. So, pleasurable feelings are highly ephemeral, and therefore unsatisfactory. This is the suffering of conditioned states.

Again, to what extent can you keep your wealth intact? Its nature is to diminish. It can be destroyed in no time if circumstances so conspire. Even if your wealth stays with you, what about your health and ability to enjoy it? If you should go blind now, what use to you is the greatest show on earth? It is the same with all your senses. Anyway, you are going to leave all your wealth behind when you die, so you wish for continued enjoyment in future existences. You try to perpetuate pleasure by acquiring merit. You do acts of merit—giving charity, keeping precepts, cultivating concentration for calm. All of these actions are efforts aimed at maintaining pleasure in perpetuity. So even a bhikkhu makes efforts just to perpetuate the suffering of rebirth, not to speak of a lay person keeping the precepts. Making a living is also full of trouble. Hankering after the heart's desire is full of trouble. The trouble is compounded if one uses improper means to get what one wants. Misdeeds open the gates of hell for one who resorts to them. These are the hazards of feeling.

The Satisfaction and Danger in Perception

The satisfaction in perception is particularly great. How is it great? Perception bestows one with certain aptitudes and propensities. It may enable one to become highly skilled, even to become a genius, but this accomplishment may be one's undoing because one is apt to be highly conceited. Perception fills one with preconceived ideas and biases. Puffed up with success, one is led into believing that one possesses the world when, in fact, one is possessed by the world. The satisfaction in perception pushes one down into the quagmire of sensuality, from where one sinks to the depths of hell.

The danger of perception lies in its transience. It is only when some agreeable thing is happening that the perception of well-being can be felt. Otherwise, the perception of enjoyment is not available. Sense objects are never stable. They do not please one constantly. Therein lies the danger of perception. For detailed arguments, what has been said about feeling applies here too.

The Satisfaction and Danger in Mental Formations

When you see a visible object, it may be either agreeable or disagreeable to you. This is "feeling originating in eye-contact." When you hear a sound, it may be either agreeable or disagreeable to you. This is "feeling originating in ear-contact." Similarly, smell causes "feeling originating in nose-contact," taste causes "feeling originating in tongue-contact," touch causes "feeling originating in body-contact," and thought causes "feeling originating in mind-contact." Personality view takes all those phenomena as "I," but right view realizes that they are merely phenomena.

It is only when same agreeable object contacts one of the six sense bases that pleasant feeling can arise. Only then can pleasant perception arise. The moment contact is broken, the pleasant feeling and the pleasant perception cease and perish. It is quite observable how you feel pleasure or displeasure through a certain contact at any of the sense bases. Observe them then, and you can probably understand their pleasant aspect and their dangers.

So, ultimately, everyone is hankering after some contact for which they have a fancy, some agreeable contact at the six sense bases, which they regard as pleasant. The world includes humans and also animals.

The Analogy of the Robot

Let me illustrate the arising and cessation of the aggregate of mental formations. Imagine a robot the size of man contrived by the supernormal powers of a man who has, through concentration, mastered the supernormal knowledge regarding phenomena. By means of his powers he has given his robot six sensitive bases that respond to six mirrors, one for each sense door. So when the mirror for the eye is focused onto the eyes of the robot, the robot's sensitivity at its eye-door and at its heart-base react to it simultaneously. The mechanism that controls the parts responds in harmony. In this way the robot stands, sits, or walks like a man. When the special mirror is withdrawn, the motion of the robot stops abruptly. For the motive force within the robot, available only through contact with the mirror that is outside the robot, is dead when the necessary contact is broken. The robot is now a piece of hardware only. The same experiment with the remaining five sense doors can be imagined.

From the analogy of the robot we should understand these facts. If the mirror were focused on the robot for the whole day, the robot would keep moving like a man the whole day. The robot has no life, and neither has the mirror. The reaction aroused within the robot's body, on contact with the mirror at the appropriate sense base, is a distinct, separate phenomenon. It does not belong to the robot, nor does it belong to the mirror. The robot's eye-door cannot produce the sensitivity by itself, neither can the mirror. Both are dead things with certain qualities only. The mechanical contrivance of the robot is like the material phenomena in us. The mirrors are like the six external sense objects. The sensitivity that is being activated within the robot is like the four mental aggregates.

In cultivating insight for right view, forget the person, or even the human shape. Concentrate only on the phenomena that rise and fall. Focus on the elements that find expression in the body.

> Phenomena arise and cease due to a given set of conditions. When those conditions cease, the arising of the particular phenomenon ceases.

When conditions prevail for the arising of desire, desire arises at the heart-base. This replaces all the previous physical phenomena in the body. All mental and physical phenomena including the materiality originating in kamma, temperature, nutriment, and consciousness undergo a change from the arising of desire.

Imagine a mine exploding in a pond and the violent impact caused to the water. Apply the underlying principle of the explosion and the water, when some strong emotion arises. Doing it fruitfully is not easy, but that is the way. Strive hard. Success depends on three factors: the example has to be appropriate, the mental and physical phenomena must be observed as they really are (unbiased by perceptions of personality or shape), and the experience must be strong enough to be observed. For instance, when strong passion arises, its arising may be observed from a detached observer's view, and the example of the mine explosion brought to bear upon it.

As greed arises, the expression on a person's face can be noticed by a careful observer. The expression is the manifestation of the new materiality that has arisen in that person. In other words, the mental phenomenon of greed can be inferred from the physical expression. If one reflects on one's own mind, the arising of a new frame of mind caused by some emotion, like greed for instance, is only too evident. When the object of greed has been enjoyed (say, a delicious meal has been eaten), or when it disappears, or if one reflects on its disgusting aspect, the greed vanishes like the ebbing of the tide in a narrow creek. The vanishing of the volition of greed is quite evident. This is how greed, a mental formation, sometimes arises within a person and how it ceases.

A warning here: do not confuse the phenomena with the personality. Focus on greed as a distinct phenomenon, not as belonging to a person. When one volition is seen through, the other volitions can be understood. All volitions arise and cease in much the same way—conceit, malice, covetousness, for instance— as and when the necessary conditions prevail. It is observable when one's spirits rise and one is ready to exert. One sees the arising of the volition of effort, and the cessation later. Likewise with the arising and cessation of delight, or the desire to do something, such as, "I want to go, but not now," or "I want to do this, but not just yet," etc. The pure volitions like confidence, generosity, or mindfulness, and the acts of charity, virtue, or meditation expressing those volitions, can also be observed.

Whenever the arising and cessation of one distinct volition is closely observed within oneself, contemplate on the fresh arisings and cessations of the aggregate of materiality.

Remember the tank of water. Also, remember the explosion in the pond. The analogies must be clear to you. The process of arising and cessation taking place in all phenomena must be clear too. The cessation of a certain element is called its impermanence. When the psychophysical phenomena in the body undergo a change, it is cessation and death. Try to visualize that death taking place in you every moment. Never despair if you have not been successful in your effort. You have to strive until you gain the right view.

As for the practice leading to the cessation of the four mental aggregates, the approach does not differ much from what was said regarding materiality. One contemplates the aggregate of materiality to gain right view about physical phenomena. One should contemplate the mental aggregates to gain right view regarding mental phenomena. The remaining factors of the Eightfold Path pave the way for right view, which is crucial.

The Danger of Impermanence in the Five Aggregates

The satisfaction and danger that lie in the aggregates of materiality, feeling, and perception have been discussed above. The danger characterized by impermanence, unsatisfactoriness, and instability is crucial for a clear understanding. Skill in the two aspects of the arising and cessation of phenomena is the proper way to understand the dangers lurking in all the aggregates of existence. Of the three forms of danger, that of impermanence is the key because once that is grasped the other two will become evident. So I shall dwell further on impermanence, which underlies the truth of the cessation of all conditioned phenomena.

Among the eleven fires[5] that constantly burn all mental and physical phenomena, the fire of death, which is the abiding danger of death, is subtle. It is not seen with the physical eye. Its heat is not tangible. Yet it burns inexorably within us and consumes all mental and physical phenomena, which is obvious. This fire is far more pervasive and greater than any conflagration on earth. It extends as far as the infinite universe and it endures as long as the endless cycle of rebirths.

I shall expand on the analogy of the flame and the fuel. The flame in the shape of the human body is a composite of eight kinds of inseparable material qualities *(aṭṭhakalāpa)*. However, not all the eight can be called fire. Visible form characterized by colour is the material element called *vaṇṇa,* but it is not fire. The primary element of extension provides the basis for the fire, but it is not fire. What holds materiality together is the element of cohesion, but it is not fire. The motion of the flame is the element of motion, but it is not fire. The smell of any object is the quality of odour *(gandha),* but it is not fire. The taste of any object is the quality of taste *(rasa),* but it is not fire. The nutrition in any object is the quality of nutritive essence *(oja),* but it is not fire. The element of fire is a separate phenomenon, which can be felt by touch. Most Buddhists are familiar with the above eight material elements. However, very few understand that each is a distinct phenomenon. Understanding them as such is important.

So, of the eight inseparable material qualities, only one is the phenomenon called fire, the other seven are its fuel. The fire is sustained by those seven kinds of fuel. As one contemplates hard on physical phenomena, the startlingly rapid succession of fresh materiality that appears is the phenomenon called arising. Wherever new materiality arises, the old materiality has been consumed. Thus all materiality that has arisen a moment ago vanishes. This vanishing is the phenomenon of death, which must not be confused with the phenomenon of burning. It is the function of fire to burn, but the function of death is to vanish

5 The eleven fires are: (i) lust *(rāga),* (ii) hatred, anger, or ill-will *(dosa),* (iii) delusion *(moha),* (iv) birth *(jāti),* (v) aging or decay *(jarā),* (vi) death *(maraṇa),* (vii) grief *(soka),* (viii) lamentation *(parideva),* (ix) physical pain *(dukkha),* (x) sorrow or mental pain *(domanassa),* and (xi) despair *(upāyāsa).*

after having arisen. The primary element of heat, which has the specific quality of burning, consumes or burns up the other seven material qualities, which always occur together. The "fire of death" (metaphorically) consumes not only its conascent seven material qualities, but also consumes the primary element of heat. The element of heat has the "burning" quality, as distinct from the phenomenon of death, which has the "vanishing" quality. This distinction is stressed here.

An Illustration

The human body is like the flame. All material elements from the smallest atom to the great earth itself are flames. All living things from the tiniest flea to the Akaniṭṭha Brahmā are flames. The flames are governed by the element of heat. All objects, animate or inanimate, are governed by the phenomenon of death, or the "fire" of death. In the flame (whether big or small) seven of the eight kinds of materiality are the fuel that is constantly being consumed by the element of fire, the eighth quality. All materiality, animate or inanimate, is fuel to the fire of death. The bodies of all beings, all vegetation, all material objects, are like burning cinders, blazing flames, or furnaces of the fire of death. All of them are the fires of the heat element too, one of the four factors that sustain materiality. However, the element of heat has the quality of variation in temperature. So this quality is the underlying phenomenon in all changes in temperature. The whole body is both cold and hot inside. The cold is conducive to cold materiality; the heat is conducive to hot materiality. The nutrition derived from our daily meals is the fuel for the element of heat inside our body. While there is nutriment in the stomach, the element of heat is kept burning inside the body, causing fresh materiality to arise.

Bodily movement causes a faster arising of fresh materiality. If one observes mindfully (a prerequisite for knowledge) as one walks, one can perceive the materiality within the whole body being powerfully agitated (like lightning or an explosion) and the fresh materiality arising with startling rapidity. No sooner has fresh materiality arisen than its cessation follows. This arising and cessation can be felt if one focuses attention on the body while walking. These successive fresh elements of materiality are ephemeral—they arise while walking is taking place. Focus your attention on the moving body to realize the phenomena at the point of arising and vanishing. Fresh materiality arises only when the previous materiality has vanished. In other bodily movements and postures the same phenomena can be observed. What people describe as, "My back is stiff," or "My legs are tired," etc., are the manifestations of rapidly changing materiality. Old materiality is constantly perishing where fresh materiality is arising.

Changes in the body due to food, change of season, illness, or cuts and bruises, are superficially noticed by everybody, but lacking insight, most people just think, "My body hurts," or "I feel ill," etc. The personal identification of phenomena with a vague sense of "I" always predominates for the average person. This persistent belief has the dire potential of pushing one down to the lower realms of existence.

It is only by gaining right view that this liability to fall into the lower realms can be prevented. Right view must be cultivated because personality view is inherent in most people. It is, so to speak, built into their very system. It can, however, be uprooted with due diligence. When a house is on fire, the owner of the house will be careful to see that every flame is put out. He will not rest until he has extinguished the last trace of fire, since even an ember can flare up at any time and consume the house. Similarly, if you want to be safe from the lower realms, you need to be diligent, constantly checking that personality view does not linger in you regarding the physical or mental phenomena occurring within you. Through repeated moments of right view, insight will develop, which is the only effective weapon against personality view.

The Analogy of the Fire-Worshipper

Personality view is not just ordinary wrong view, but the gravest wrong view. There is, for instance, the wrong view of fire-worship. When a child is born, the fire-worshipper's parents kindle a fire for the child. For sixteen years the parents keep the fire alive by refuelling it regularly with ghee or butter. When he is sixteen, the parents ask their son whether he will remain as a layman or become a recluse and take up the practice that will lead him to the brahmā realm. If the boy chooses to become a recluse, the parents hand over the sacrificial fire to him. The recluse then takes upon himself the duty of feeding the fire with the best ghee or butter. The purer the fuel, the more meritorious is the fire-sacrifice. He takes the sacrificial fire wherever he goes. He keeps the flame alight constantly throughout his life. By this dutiful sacrifice he earns merit said to lead to rebirth in the brahmā world. This fire-worshipper is virtually a slave to his sacrificial fire. For as long as he lives, maybe a hundred years or more, his servitude persists. For as long as his wrong belief in the virtue of the fire sacrifice persists, he will serve the fire dutifully. This is, of course, a case of *saṅkhāra dukkha,* the tyranny of conditioned states. It is the nature of fire to consume whatever fuel it can lay hold of. Searching for fuel to keep the fire alive is therefore never-ending serfdom, eternal suffering.

The analogy of the fire-worshipper is this: All beings who have strong attachment to "self," which is but the five aggregates, exhaust themselves to maintain their lives, but they are only feeding the fire that consumes from within. The fire of death is kept alive, consuming fresh materiality and mentality, being sustained by regular feeding.

All Beings are Fuel to the Fire of Death

Human existence is fuel for the fire of human death. A deva's existence is fuel for the fire of a deva's death. A brahmā's existence is fuel for the fire of a brahmā's death. Almsgiving done to acquire merit for these forms of existence is merely trouble taken to feed the fires of these existences. It virtually means cultivating the fields where these fires are to thrive. Keeping the precepts to acquire merit—whether five, eight, or ten precepts—is merely cultivating the field to reap a good crop of fires. Similarly, developing concentration or the four divine abidings is merely cultivating the field of fires. In the beginningless cycle of rebirths, every being has done infinite deeds of giving, and has reaped the results of infinite existences as human beings or as devas. All of those existences have been consumed by the fire of death. Not a particle of ash remains. In each of these existences, the nurturing of one's life, from the time one could look after oneself until death, is just feeding the fire of death. Nothing remains at the time of death. There is no fundamental difference between such subsistence and maintaining the sacrificial fire of the fire-worshipping recluse.

This analogy is given to drive home the truth of the impermanence of all materiality, the danger that besets all living beings.

Try to Understand the Phenomenon of Death

In spite of the inevitability of death, most people usually ignore it. You should meditate to realize the omnipresence of death. Try to visualize the ceaseless burning of the fire of death in all the four postures: standing, sitting, walking, and lying down.

All the merits acquired in the past through giving, virtue, or meditation for calm, if they were aimed at prolonging existence, are futile. The acquisition of merit now aimed at prolonging existence in the future will lead to the same fate. The burdensome tasks that one undertakes to support one's present existence are no different either. All these efforts merely serve as fuel for the fire of death. This is to impress upon you the futility of all human efforts, however meritorious, aimed at the continuation of existence.

The Five Aggregates and the Four Noble Truths

The five aggregates, being truly impermanent, are unsatisfactory. This is the Noble Truth of Suffering. Attachment to the five aggregates as one's own property, or one's own self, and the craving for existence and rebirth, is the origin of suffering. This is the Noble Truth of the Cause of Suffering. The liberation from craving, which is the same as the escape from the five aggregates, is the Noble Truth of the Cessation of Suffering. The Noble Eightfold Path beginning with right view is the Noble Truth of the Path Leading to the Cessation of Suffering.

Chapter Three

The third question relates to nibbāna—its nature, the zeal, happiness, and peace that its attainment holds, and the development of the recollection of the tranquillity of nibbāna *(upasamānussati)*.

The Element of Deliverance

Regarding your request about the recollection of nibbāna, it is an exercise that properly belongs to the Noble Ones only, who have realized nibbāna and experienced its peace. So it is not a relevant meditation practice for you, Maung Thaw. You have not realized nibbāna yourself and the peace of nibbāna is understood only on its realization. What it would mean to those who have realized it is therefore conjecture, and conjecture is not mental development. I believe you have some degree of peace pertaining to nibbāna, but it is only temporary; it is not yet a distinct element to be reflected on by way of mental development. It is shrouded by defilements both before and after it. However, a recollection on the peace of nibbāna, even conjecturally, is highly worthwhile, so I will give a reply that should help you to think on the right lines.

We have seen how realization of the dangers in the five aggregates brings about the cessation of craving, which is the origin of all ill. That is the nature of peace *(santi)*, which is nibbāna. It is also the escape from the five aggregates of existence.

The analogy of the fire-worshipper illustrates the folly of ignorant people who fail to grasp the dangers of impermanence and death—the two great fires that consume all forms of existence. There is such a thing as the quelling of those two fires, which is peace. If you fail to see death as a distinct phenomenon, it is impossible to understand what is meant by escape from existence, the element of deliverance. It is only when sufficient insight is gained into the real nature of death as a phenomenon, that the significance of deliverance may be realized.

> In the endless round of rebirth there is never such a thing as a person or a self; there are only elements and their phenomena.

If you watch the waters of a river and contemplate well, you will understand how the cold element (which is only an aspect of the element of heat) merges with other material qualities and flows on, always changing. In the eternal cycle of rebirth there is only an endless stream of phenomena, the five aggregates of existence, incessantly flowing like the waters of a river, and no person or self ever exists. If the fertile element of craving, the origin of all existence, prevails in the five aggregates, this cycle of rebirth will go on without end, and no escape is in sight.

When right view arises and realizes the true nature of existence, supramundane insight knowledge extinguishes craving instantly. This extinction of craving is the element of deliverance. Distinguish between death and deliverance. Death is the voracious fire that consumes all materiality and mentality. Deliverance is the coolness, the calm, the peace, that allays and quenches the fire of death. This element of deliverance is unique since it is not dependent on, or associated with, any other element for its existence. Just as the sky cannot be burnt by fire, washed away by water, or destroyed by any other means, so too the element of deliverance, being extremely subtle, is not affected by the fires of birth, decay, death, lust, hatred, or delusion. It is the fire-exit or escape from the eleven fires that constantly burn all beings who have not realized it. Since it has no birth, there is no beginning to it. It cannot be identified or counted. Being deathless, there is no end to it.

> "This phenomenon of release is intelligible only by supramundane insight, it is indefinable, it is infinite: its luminosity surpasses the sun at its brightest."[6]

---

6 *Brahmanimantana Sutta, Mūlapaṇṇāsa, Majjhimanikāya, Sutta* 49.

In the above quotation, "intelligible only by supramundane insight" connotes the peace perceived through attainment to supramundane knowledge. The reality of the fire of death and other fires such as lust, hatred, delusion, birth and aging, has to be properly understood, and the moment it is understood, its antithesis of calm, tranquillity, or peace is realized.

"Indefinable" means that it cannot be said when it began or when it will end, or when it arises or does not arise. It cannot be said where it exists, or at which point it is present. It cannot be identified as, "This is the peace of such and such a Buddha, of such and such a Solitary Buddha, of such and such an Arahant." It cannot be classified as superior or inferior, such as, "The peace of a Buddha excels that of other Arahants," etc. Put in another way, the peace of the Buddha and that of Khujjuttarā the maid who became an Arahant cannot be distinguished.

"Infinite" means the peace realized by the Arahants throughout saṃsāra cannot be arranged in chronological order.

"Luminous" means that in all the three mundane realms mentioned above, the fire of death glows fiercely. Throughout saṃsāra, countless existences have been devoured by this fire, and it is still burning voraciously. For the indefinite future too, this fire will go on burning, consuming all phenomena that arise. The fear of death is universal. Such is the intensity of the fire of death. In the supramundane sphere, the Dhamma shines that is called the element of deliverance or release. Remember the radiant peace attained to by innumerable Buddhas, Solitary Buddhas, Chief Disciples, and Disciples.

This is a brief attempt at describing nibbāna which defies description.

The True Peace of Nibbāna

Regarding your query about how a person attaining nibbāna finds peace, the answer is that nibbāna is not found by any person. This is simply because nibbāna is, whereas a person or a self is not. Only phenomena, and no being or soul exists.

In discussing nibbāna it is vital not to confuse actuality with concept. The average person, i.e. one who has not gained insight, is full of preconceived notions, ideas, and ideologies, and is apt to be led astray by them. One's own ideas of peace usually dominate. For instance, there is the solidity of the body. If one fails to see the material quality of extension, which is manifested as solidity or support, one will simply think that it is the solidity of one's own body. So one is still an ignorant person. One is unable to understand real peace, for real peace does not belong to a person. It is never one's own peace or the peace that one enjoys. Similarly, the elements of cohesion, heat, motion, greed, anger, etc., need to be understood in the ultimate sense, if one is to comprehend nibbāna.

Aging and death are common to all. If one thinks that one has grown old, or that one must die one day, that is just common mundane knowledge. Because of the dreadful, false "I" concept, one loathes aging as happening to one's person. One fears death only because one holds tenaciously onto existence, which one calls one's life. Overwhelmed by this craving for existence, one fails to understand death as a distinct phenomenon. Unless one knows it as such, one is an ignorant person incapable of understanding nibbāna. One can talk accurately about nibbāna only when one has discarded personality view and gained the right view into elements and phenomena.

The flux of phenomena, ever perpetuating the cycle of rebirth, is just a series of arising and cessation, births and deaths, that occur thousands of times within a blink of the eyes. The process is incessant and inexorable. Since the twin root causes of ignorance and craving are present, this incessant perishing of gross phenomena takes place, consumed by the eleven fires within oneself. At death, the process continues as a fresh existence in one of the three realms, accompanied by the eleven fires. When ignorance and craving are extinguished, then the mental and physical aggregates in that existence do not continue as a fresh existence. The extinction of the eleven fires is the escape from the clutches of death. Whereas the compounded existence of elements is conventionally called a being, when the "being" has realized the element of deliverance or peace, that element itself might be called the one who has attained nibbāna (parinibbāna).

Just because saṃsāra is beginningless and endless, one should not have any concept of time regarding nibbāna. Again, just because innumerable Buddhas, Solitary Buddhas, and Noble Disciples have entered parinibbāna, one should not associate nibbāna with numbers.

The idea of the endless cycle of rebirth pertains only to mental and material phenomena that are subject to the process of arising and cessation, or momentary births and deaths. Don't let that lengthy process linger in your mind when you consider nibbāna. For nibbāna is real, whereas time is a concept. Saṃsāra is infinite, but nibbāna cannot be said to have any beginning at all. One is apt to get confused since nibbāna is the very antithesis of saṃsāra. Saṃsāra is an endless process that defies measurement. Nibbāna exists in the ultimate sense, whereas the existences of beings are always changing and do not remain for a moment. Do not think of nibbāna with any reference to the transient world. Do not wonder about the present location of the former Noble Ones. For example, as a train moves along, trees at a distance seem to be moving along with it, but in fact the trees are stationary. Similarly, saṃsāra moves on like the train, but nibbāna is motionless like the distant trees. The reflection of the moon at its zenith would appear in every tray of water, if trays were placed in every house in Asia. The number of moons reflected in the trays has nothing to do with the actual moon. The reflections are like those who have passed on to nibbāna, and nibbāna is like the moon.

This, then, is a short explanation about nibbāna or deliverance, with particular emphasis on the fact that nibbāna is not for any "person" to enter. This is the answer to the third question. Plenty of treatises on nibbāna have been written by learned scholars. Here, only a résumé has been given on this vast subject.

Chapter Four

The fourth question asks about the way that would lead a blind worldling *(andhaputhujjana)* on to the level of a wise and virtuous ordinary person *(kalyāṇaputhujjana)*.[7]

Two Types of Ordinary Person

> "The Buddha, the kinsman of the sun, speaks of two types of ordinary person: the blind worldling and the wise and virtuous ordinary person."
>
> (Paṭisambhidāmagga Commentary)

The Blind Worldling

> "One who has no scriptural learning, being without knowledge of the aggregates, the elements, the twelve sense bases, dependent origination, the foundations of mindfulness, etc., or the interpretation and discrimination thereof that can prevent the arising of personality view, is a blind worldling."
> (Mūlapaṇṇāsa Commentary)

The Wise and Virtuous Ordinary Person

> "One who is learned regarding the five aggregates, the twelve sense bases, the eighteen elements, in the original Pāḷi, can

7 A *puthujjana* is an ordinary, unenlightened person as opposed to a Noble One or *ariya*. *Andha* means blind, *kalyāṇa* means skilful or wise.

interpret it correctly, and can discriminate each item by means of examples, illustrations, anecdotes, etc., and has therefore gained a thorough knowledge of those teachings is a wise and virtuous ordinary person." (ibid.)

"Likewise, one who has gained a thorough knowledge of the twelve links in the chain of dependent origination, the four foundations of mindfulness, the four right efforts, the four bases of success, the five controlling faculties, the five powers, the seven factors of enlightenment, and the eight factors of the Noble Path, is called a wise or virtuous ordinary person. Such knowledge is a characteristic of a virtuous ordinary person." (ibid.)

One who lacks this eye of the Dhamma, even a ruler of the celestial worlds with the divine eye, is called a blind worldling. One who is proficient in the seven aspects in the five aggregates qualifies as a wise person. How?

Proficiency in the first aspect is thorough knowledge of the four primary elements, the five aggregates, and the twelve sense bases.

Proficiency in the second and third aspects—the arising and cessation of phenomena, thus, "Owing to the arising of nutriment, materiality arises; owing to the cessation or exhaustion of nutriment, materiality ceases. Owing to the arising of contact, feeling arises; owing to the cessation of contact, feeling ceases" covers part of the law of dependent origination.

Proficiency in the fourth aspect, i.e., the Noble Eightfold Path, covers the thirty-seven factors of enlightenment, the threefold training of higher virtue, higher concentration, and higher understanding, the ten perfections, and the Four Noble Truths. Of the eight factors of the Noble Path, right view and right thought are called higher understanding; right speech, right action, and right livelihood are called higher virtue; right effort, right mindfulness, and right concentration are called higher concentration.

As for the ten perfections: giving, virtue, patience, and truthfulness constitute higher virtue; renunciation is the right thought as to the dangerous and disgusting nature of sensuality, loving-kindness is right thought as non-malice; resolve and equanimity are in full accord with right concentration; wisdom means right view, and energy is right effort. This is how the ten perfections are included in the virtuous person's knowledge. A wise and virtuous ordinary person is also called a lesser stream-winner *(cūḷa-sotāpanna)*.

If the virtuous ordinary person can develop knowledge to the supramundane level by gaining insight into the seven aspects, he or she is bound to become a fully-fledged stream-winner. One can then advance in the attainment of the path knowledges until one becomes an Arahant. All these are possible right now.

> "Bhikkhus, a bhikkhu who earnestly wants to understand the true nature of materiality to eradicate the defilements, who habitually contemplates materiality from three approaches, who is proficient in the seven aspects of materiality is, in this Dhamma and Discipline, called accomplished, one who has lived the life, a perfect one or an excellent man."

Chapter Five

The fifth request is a question of assimilation. "The Buddha said that nothing falls outside the scope of the Four Noble Truths, and that nothing cannot be employed as a fruitful subject for contemplation. Would the Venerable Sayādaw kindly give us a guide to the practical application of the Dhamma so that, when we do any meritorious deed, we can be mindful of the Four Noble Truths and the three characteristics of impermanence, unsatisfactoriness, and not-self, thus fulfilling the threefold training, cultivating the ten perfections and simultaneously bearing in mind dependent origination, and the twenty-four conditional relations?"

How to be Mindful while Doing a Meritorious Deed

I shall now explain briefly how a single utterance of "*Buddhaṃ saraṇaṃ gacchāmi*—I go to the Buddha as my refuge," is an act of merit that encompasses the Four Noble Truths, the three characteristics of existence, the fulfilment of the threefold training, and the cultivation of the ten perfections, done while one is mindful of dependent origination and the twenty-four conditional relations.

In uttering the words "*Buddhaṃ saraṇaṃ gacchāmi,*" by the time you have uttered the last syllable, a great moral consciousness, accompanied by joy and connected with knowledge, has arisen. This impulsion is good kamma of the highest class accompanied by three wholesome roots: non-greed, non-hatred, and non-delusion. The impulsion lasts for seven thought-moments. Each of the seven thought-moments[8] comprises the four mental aggregates: feeling, perception, mental formations, and consciousness. The impulsion from that produces material quality of sound audible to the ear as "Buddhaṃ saraṇaṃ gacchāmi." Thus we see how the five aggregates arise. There is also the material phenomena present at the heart-base, the source of the impulsive mental activities pervading the whole body.

As to mindfulness of the Four Noble Truths: By the time the last syllable has been uttered, the five aggregates are being consumed by the ever-present fire of death, which is the truth of suffering. Remember the danger in the five aggregates: "The transience, unsatisfactoriness, and instability of materiality, constitute the danger in materiality (see p.37).

The nutriment that has been producing the aggregate of materiality during the utterance is the truth of the origin of materiality. The contact arisen from the mental object of the Buddha's noble attributes is the origin of the arising of feeling, perception, and mental formations—the truth of the cause in respect of the mental aggregates. The three mental aggregates and the heart-base are the truth of the origin of consciousness. As soon as the recollection of the Buddha arises in your mind, the three basic evils of greed, hatred and delusion are destroyed, which is the truth of cessation, or momentary bliss.[9] The five factors of the Noble Eightfold Path involved in impulsion, namely, right view, right thought, right effort, right mindfulness, and right concentration, are mindfulness of the Noble Eightfold Path. This is how the Four Noble Truths are realized in a single utterance while recollecting the Buddha.

The Three Characteristics of Existence

Remember our previous example of the robot. Herein, the mind-object, the Buddha's attributes, is like the mirror. This mirror is focused on the heart-base of the robot, which instantly receives the mental object and apperceives it. Seven thought-moments of

---

8 A process of sense cognition consists of seventeen thought-moments, of which seven arise at the stage of impulsion *(javana)*.

9 Of the two sets of *samudaya* and *nirodha* mentioned above (p.31), it is the *samudaya* and *nirodha* of the present existence that is relevant here.

impulsion flash out from the heart-base—seven highly-charged mental activities that cause verbal action to arise through its motive power, comparable to the agitated waters when a mine explodes in a pond or like the whistling of the steamer.

The example of the agitated water is analogous to materiality being agitated. However, impulsion is so inconceivably rapid that no adequate example can be given. The power of impulsion over all materiality in your body must be perceived in every activity. If this is not clearly perceived, the danger of hell remains. If you really dread the fires of hell, it is well to cultivate insight to perceive the change of materiality caused by impulsion.

The example of the water tank best illustrates the rapidity of change in physical phenomena as impulsion arises. The transience of materiality, the decaying and the fresh arising within the whole body, may not be vivid enough even by means of that analogy.

So let's take another example. Imagine a life-size doll made of cotton-wool. Soak it in spirit and burn it. Observe how quickly the cotton-wool changes from one end to the other. The changes within the body may not be as clearly noticeable as in the burning doll, being many times faster. Don't despair, though. When a flame is kindled in a dark room, the darkness in the entire room vanishes the instant that light arises, and the light fills the whole room at once. In this example, light is new materiality originating in the flame. It arises so swiftly that one cannot follow it with the eye. You only know its arising by seeing the lighted room. So too, you cannot actually observe the cessation of darkness, but you can know that it has ceased. The change of materiality within your body is the same. Its rapidity need not be a barrier to your understanding. The fact of change is inescapable to your vigilant consciousness and can be known. That is the nature of insight. The rapidity of the change of psychophysical phenomena is not even known by the Noble Disciples. Only the Buddhas can trace it. As for disciples, the abandonment of personality view through insight into impermanence is sufficient for enlightenment.

As soon as the utterance of "*Buddhaṃ saraṇaṃ gacchāmi*" has ended, the flashes of impulsion vanish in the heart-base so that all materiality actuated by that impulsion ceases, just as when a flame is extinguished in a dark room all the light suddenly disappears.

When the thought of the Buddha vanishes with its concomitant mental activities, other forms of consciousness, depending on the mind-object, take over. This is also observable.

The knowledge that understands the cessation of the four mental aggregates and the materiality dependent on them is called knowledge of impermanence. The cessation of phenomena must be discerned. Merely saying "impermanent, impermanent" is not insight, nor is it mental development. Once the truth of impermanence is grasped, the painful fact that all mental and physical phenomena merely feed the fires of death will be clearly realized. Then the relevance of the analogy of the fire-worshipper will be fully appreciated. When the perpetual arising and cessation of all phenomena within oneself is clearly perceived, the illusion of "I" will fall away. You will then understand that the phenomena are never you or your self. The characteristic of anattā is discerned only in this manner. If lack of a self is not perceived, all talk of anatta is fruitless. It is not knowledge, it is not insight, it is not practice for mental development.

The Threefold Training

Of the threefold training, the volition that impels a person to utter the words, "*Buddhaṃ saraṇaṃ gacchāmi,*" belongs to higher virtue because it is a virtuous act motivated by a conscious undertaking to abstain from the four kinds of immoral speech. That volition comprises right effort, right mindfulness and right concentration—the three factors of higher concentration. Right view and right thought in uttering the words constitute higher understanding.

The Ten Perfections

Understand the practice of the perfections in the manner of the Noble Eightfold Path discussed above.

Regarding Dependent Origination

The second aspect discussed concerning the virtuous person is, in essence, dependent origination. Nutriment arising, materiality arises; contact arising, feeling arises; perception arising, mental formations arise; psychophysical phenomena arising, consciousness arises. Tracing the cause in this way by analysing the results is the Buddha's method of teaching called dependent origination.

As to the twenty-four types of conditional relations, I shall not give a reply here for these reasons: (i) it is probably too abstract for you, Maung Thaw; (ii) it is not useful for insight training; (iii) it is purely for the finer discriminations to be exercised by those who have attained to path knowledge. When you have digested the present answers, you may ask for it later.

Chapter Six

The sixth request pertains to the Buddha's victory over the five māras; the definition, characteristics and significance of the five māras; and the difference between the body of Prince Siddhattha, the bodhisatta, and that of the Buddha. Here are my answers:

The Five Māras

1. *Māra Devaputta*, the celestial villain of the sixth devaloka, the "Tempter" and the embodiment of evil.
2. *Kilesas*, the ten defilements.
3. *Abhisaṅkhāra*, kamma or volitional action.
4. *Khandha*, continued existence.
5. *Maccu*, death.

By "māra" is meant "the killer." The world is ravaged by five killers. The first one is the evil deva whose abode is in Paranimittavasavattī Devaloka. His hordes are not only in his celestial abode, but spread all over, including the human abode.

Buddha's Victory over Māra Devaputta

Many people adhere to wrong beliefs. To escape from such a perverse world one has to face opposition from such people. Seeing the bodhisatta seated on the throne of victory, firmly resolved[10] to remain until he won enlightenment, Māra could not

10 (i) "Let my skin remain, let my sinews remain, let my bones remain, let

leave him unopposed. He had to try to foil him, for he had often failed. He mustered all his forces and attacked the bodhisatta. He roused storms that toppled mountain tops. He employed all his means of destruction but without success. His forces spent, he approached the Buddha and made false claims on the throne of victory, not really wanting it but merely to harass the Buddha.

The Buddha told him that the throne of victory arose from the accumulation of his perfections fulfilled, but what perfections had Māra practised? Māra referred to his followers in witness of his right. The Buddha was alone then, since all the celestial beings had fled. So the Buddha touched the earth to bear witness to the deeds of giving he had practised when he had poured the ceremonial water onto the earth. At that instant the great earth trembled and the skies rumbled, sending Māra and his impressive army helter-skelter. Then Māra accepted defeat and returned to his celestial abode. This, in brief, is the Buddha's victory over Māra Devaputta.

Victory over Defilements and Volitional Actions

On attaining the path knowledge of Arahantship the Buddha gained a victory over all the defilements. The volitional actions that manifest only in association with the defilements also died a natural death. Volitional actions, good or bad, are called abhisaṅkhāra, one of the five "killers." These actions do not germinate as fresh becoming when deprived of craving, for once the craving for existence is gone, kamma loses its potential to reproduce, just like boiled grains. With the exhaustion of greed, hatred, and delusion, all immoral actions cease absolutely. All moral actions do not have kammic force in them and remain inoperative *(kiriya)*. This is how victory over defilements and volitional action was won by the Buddha.

What remained was the five aggregates, which were the result of kamma done before the defilements were extinguished, and psychophysical phenomena due to the four causes[11] before enlightenment, but free from defilements since then. The existence

---

my blood dry up, (ii) let the earth turn upside down; (iii) let tens of thousands of thunderbolts strike my head; (iv) let this Uruvela Forest catch fire and be reduced to cinders, I will not rise till I win enlightenment."

11 Kamma, consciousness, temperature, and nutriment.

of the five aggregates presupposes the results of past actions, both wholesome and unwholesome. This occurrence of results continued until the moment of the Buddha's passing away. Since the five aggregates still existed after his enlightenment, the effects of past kamma were felt. In other words, because the kammic forces of the past still remained, the five aggregates persisted. The existence of the Buddha's five aggregates allowed the release of the multitude from suffering.

This is stated in different ways for fear that you might make a wrong interpretation regarding the exhaustion of kammic forces.

Victory over the Five Aggregates

The Buddha's aggregate of psychophysical phenomena is called the Buddha's aggregates *(khandha)*. His parinibbāna or moment of decease is called death *(maccu)*. These two "killers" are overcome only while abiding in nibbāna or at the moment of parinibbāna. This is according to the commentaries: "On the throne of victory under the bodhi tree, only the three māras were vanquished."

A Different Interpretation in the Subcommentary

The author of the subcommentary on the Dhātukathā has a different interpretation. He says that all the five māras were vanquished on attainment of enlightenment. His explanation runs as follows:

On the first three māras, no explanation is needed. On the aggregates and death he says, "If craving, the cause of the five aggregates, is present, fresh arising of the aggregates is bound to follow. Once the truth of the cause has been realized and craving extinguished, all future existences die out automatically. Along with the extinction of future existences, the liability to death also vanishes altogether." This final extinction of all future aggregates and of the accompanying deaths, the author contends, amounts to victory over the aggregates and death, which took place on the Buddha's attaining the Eye of the Dhamma.

With respect to the present aggregates and the present death, the Buddha had vanquished them there and then because, whereas the aggregates had previously been seen as a person—thereby leading to the unfortunate cycle of rebirth—on attaining enlightenment this delusion was gone, so the aggregates could no longer oppress or "kill" him. The phenomenon of death was also understood and so death lost its sting. Thereafter no fear of death remained. No fuel remained for it to consume. Thus death was vanquished too.

Let us make an illustration. A wicked demoness who liked to feed on excrement and putridity possessed a good man. She drove him out of his senses so that the poor man was subject to her will, and he roamed about in cemeteries and such places to feed on excrement and putrefied corpses. After years of subjugation, the man was cured of the curse by a magician who brought him back to his senses. With the help of the magician's powers, i.e. by making use of the divine eye in a magic formula, he saw the demoness within him. He could now clearly assess the situation. He had conquered the demoness, but after many years of co-existence he could not drive her out at once. Besides, he saw some benefit of her presence; he could put her to his use. The extraordinary physical powers she had would be useful for his own purposes. He could perform miracles, harnessing her powers in the service of humanity.

The analogy is this. The demoness is like the five aggregates. The proper sense of the man is like the non-causative type of good deeds. Cemeteries and such places are like the three realms of existence. The divine eye, the magician's formula, is the Eye of the Dhamma. Continued upkeep of the demoness within is like the continued existence of the Buddha, which could not cease at once because it was his long-cherished wish to help the multitude in their struggle for release from suffering. In fact, the Buddha and the Noble Ones, after attaining Arahantship, live on only for the good of others.

This is how the subcommentary explains the Buddha's victories over the aggregates and death even at the time of his enlightenment.

The Five Māras Defined

1. *Māra Devaputta*: explained above.
2. *Kilesa–Māra* : The basic defilements are greed, hatred, and delusion.

3. *Abhisaṅkhāra–Māra*: The ten moral kammas and the ten immoral kammas. It also includes all volitional actions that are dependent on the cycle of rebirth such as giving, virtue, meditation, reverence, sharing one's merits, rejoicing in the merits of others, etc.
4. *Khandha–Māra*: The five aggregates manifested in the existences as humans, devas, brahmās, etc.
5. *Maccu–Māra*: Death, the phenomenon of mortality.

The Nature of the Five Māras

The word "*māra*" means "killer" or "destroyer." It destroys life in the physical sense, and also in the moral sense. Life means and includes:

1. The life-faculty *(jīvitindriya)*;
2. Pure or virtuous qualities such as confidence, morality, etc.;
3. Non-causative or non-kammic merits or practice of the ten perfections such as giving, virtue, etc.

The life-faculty means the ability to sustain an existence as water sustains the lotus. The life-faculty sustains the aggregates in each existence. When the life-faculty is destroyed, the aggregates break up and the existence ends, which we call the death of a being. Virtue is the "life" of a good person. When one's virtue is broken, one's "life" is destroyed. Although one is physically alive one is morally dead. Non-causative or non-kammic merit is the very life of a bodhisatta. Until an aspirant to Buddhahood receives formal recognition and assurance from a living Buddha, the aspiration is still in danger. For the aspirant is still susceptible to wrong views, which are the antithesis of enlightenment. One's life as a bodhisatta is thereby destroyed, and so one reverts to being an ordinary person.

The Significance of the Five Māras

Māra, the Wicked One, is the destroyer of what is virtuous in living beings. Any higher aspirations to supramundane merits are his prime objects of destruction. Therefore he is called Māra, the "destroyer."

The phenomenon of death is the destroyer of the life-faculty. It destroys all living beings, hence its name—maccu.

Defilements such as greed, hatred, delusion, conceit, wrong view, etc., destroy virtue and the aspiration for non-kammic action. Kammic actions such as almsgiving, virtue, etc., that have causative merit, inevitably cause new existences. The aggregates of existence thus produced have death as an inherent factor. Not only is the fire of death inherent, so too are the defilements, the "destroyers." That is why merits and demerits are called *abhisaṅkhārā*, the "destroyers." The five aggregates, being subject to decay, destroy the life-faculty. By harbouring the defilements, they cause the destruction of virtue and the aspiration to non-causative merit. This is how the five māras destroy.

How Defilements Destroy

To put it in a different way, take greed, for instance. Greed in a bhikkhu destroys his precepts, his dignified training, his nobility. Greed in a layman destroys his morality, his dignity, and his reputation. Again, greed in a bhikkhu destroys the real well-being of a bhikkhu that lies in forsaking worldly interests and possessions. It destroys the attainments in concentration and spiritual powers. Greed in a layman causes undue loss of property, and even loss of life, limbs or sense organs, or premature death. All these evils befall one who succumbs to greed. It is similar with hatred or anger.

In another sense, greed destroys generosity, hatred destroys kindness, delusion destroys wisdom. All the generosity practised over aeons of previous existences can be brought to nothing when one is overwhelmed by greed. Hatred and other defilements are the same. In the present existence too, occasional purity of the mind due to hearing (or reading) the Dhamma is destroyed in no time by greed. It is just like the darkness of night that nullifies all lightning flashes, however frequently they might occur. Understand the evils of hatred and other defilements likewise. This is how the defilements destroy all that is pure and virtuous in living beings.

How the Aggregates Destroy

The destructive nature of the five aggregates should be observed within oneself. Try to visualize the destruction of one of the four primary elements that you call your head. Similarly, observe your eye, ear, nose, cheek, teeth, tongue, mouth and throat, then down into your lungs and heart, etc.

Contemplate the deaths that occur due to seeking for the pleasures of desirable visible objects. Similarly, consider the deaths caused by the lure of some pleasant sound, scent, taste, or touch. All these are how materiality destroys.

Consider the deaths originating in one's pursuit of pleasant sensations born of eye-contact ... pleasant sensations born of mind-contact. All these are how feeling destroys.

Consider the deaths due to pursuit of some perception regarding visible forms ... some perception regarding mind-objects. These are how perception destroys.

Death resulting from pursuing one's faith is the destruction wrought by faith. Death resulting from keeping virtue is the destruction through virtue. Similarly, learning the Dhamma, liberality, acquisition of knowledge, and meditation are all moral volitions that can destroy. As for immoral volitions such as greed, hatred, etc., their destructiveness is obvious. All these are how mental formations destroy.

Death due to yearning for eye-consciousness is how eye-consciousness destroys ... death due to yearning for mind-consciousness is how mind-consciousness destroys. All these are how consciousness destroys. This is a brief explanation of how the four mental aggregates destroy.

How Death Destroys

Consider this, "How many of my heads have perished over the innumerable round of existences? How many eyes? How many ears? How many noses? How many tongues? How many hearts and lungs? All of them were materiality that formed the essential part of my existences."

Consider, "How many kilograms of food and drink have I so far consumed in my present existence. How many kilograms of matter that makes up my head have been consumed during my existence? All that was sustained by nutriment only. How much of the matter that makes up my eyes, my ears, my nose, my tongue, my heart, and my lungs have so far been consumed by death?"

With respect to mental phenomena, consider how many mental phenomena have perished that had arisen at the eye-base? ... that had arisen at the mind-base? In pondering thus, concentrate on the phenomenon of death, and don't let any personality view creep in. Don't associate your false "self" with either the phenomena of "the consumer" or "the consumed" (the five aggregates).

The Example of the Magic Pill

I shall illustrate the swiftness of change taking place in the five aggregates. Let us say there is a charm in the form of a pill. The pills are coloured white, red, black, etc. On throwing one—say, a white one—accompanied by the appropriate incantation, an apparition the size and weight of a man suddenly appears. It is completely white. Then, another pill—this time a red one— accompanied by the appropriate incantation, is thrown into the heart-base of the apparition. Suddenly the red colour permeates the whole body of the apparition, beginning from the heart. Wherever red takes over, the previous white vanishes, and no white can be seen. The apparition is now completely red. The colour distinction is to help visualize the change that takes place. Concentrate on the merging of the red colour into the white and how the former white disappears even before your mind's eye. This disappearance or disintegration is what is constantly happening within us.

> "Though one should live a hundred years
> not seeing the sublime Dhamma,
> better is a single day lived by one
> who sees the sublime Dhamma." (Dhp 115.)

This is an explanation of how death relentlessly destroys the life-sustaining materiality from the moment each new existence comes into being. If you understand what has been said on the dangerous aspect of the aggregates, you should find no difficulty in understanding the destructiveness that is the aggregates and death.

As to the difference in the aggregates of the Buddha before and after enlightenment: before enlightenment the five aggregates of the bodhisatta contained stains of defilements and putridity of kammic actions, while after enlightenment no trace of these stains and putridity remained. The body of one who is still training to become an Arahant, having gained the three earlier stages of enlightenment, decomposes and putrefies after death. The bodies of the Buddha and Arahants do not decompose or putrefy after their parinibbāna. The difference exists even while they are still living.

Although both the Buddha and the Arahant eat the same kind of food as non-Arahants, the purity of the aggregates of mind in the former produce materiality born of pure consciousness, which is as pure and clear as sterilized cotton-wool.

The Analogy of the Wish-Fulfilling Gem of the Universal Monarch

When the wish-fulfilling gem of the Universal Monarch is placed in a turbid pool, the waters instantly turn crystal-clear. Similarly, because the impulsions of the Buddha and the Arahants are always pure and clean, the aggregates of their bodies are perfectly pure and clean. No foul smell could arise from such materiality.

A king's palace is not worthy of worshipping while it is being occupied by a king. However, were it to be converted into a temple it would be well worthy of worship, and might be a place from which one could ascend to heaven or attain nibbāna.

The body of the bodhisatta is like the king's palace. The body of the Buddha is like the temple where the Buddha is staying. The body before enlightenment only supported the mind of Prince Siddhattha. The body since he renounced the palace to practise meditation is worth worshipping. Therefore his robes were taken and kept in Dussacetī by Suddhāvāsa Brahmā. Don't follow the wrong view that says the body is not the Buddha, only great wisdom is the Buddha.

Chapter Seven

The seventh question was, "I would like to know the method of taking refuge in the Three Gems."

How to Practise the Three Refuges

I am not going to describe the Three Gems in detail because they have been well explained in such books as the Saraṇādivinicchaya. Only the main points will be shown here.

People often think, "If I worship this teaching, it will free me from the lower realms." If these meditations have the merit needed to avoid the lower realms, then they may be called refuges. Some believe that meditating on this or that teaching will bring enough merit to avoid the lower realms. This kind of worship cannot bring such merit. It is useless. Those who believe in those teachings are not a refuge and are not worthy of respect. They are also not able to find a refuge. You must understand this while taking refuge.

To give a simile: the purified attributes of virtue, concentration, and wisdom are like fertile soil; the Noble Ones possessing those attributes are like a fertile field. Worshipping them is like sowing seed in that field. Here, the volition to worship is the seed. One who is without virtue, concentration, or wisdom, and therefore thinks only immoral thoughts, is like dry, rocky land. Worshipping one like that is just like sowing seed on barren land. The worshipper's act (however reverential) is futile and brings no merit.

Nevertheless, there are sure ways of earning merit and demerit, modes of conduct that are moral or immoral, and happy destinies or unhappy destinies understood down the ages by the wise (whether bhikkhus, laymen, or recluses). Wrong believers disregard all these merits and demerits and declare that what is meritorious is demeritorious, or that what is demeritorious is meritorious. One with such perverted views is like a burning rock. One who worships such a teacher is like one who sows seed on a burning rock. Instead of gaining merit, the worshipper will be burned.

Taking refuge is of two kinds: by hearsay and by direct knowledge. Taking refuge through blind faith in the noble attributes of the Buddha, the Dhamma, and the Saṅgha, but without right view, is by hearsay. It is so called because the act of taking refuge is not complete in so far as the worshipper has not actually "seen" the Buddha, the Dhamma, or the Saṅgha; he has not perceived the teaching; he has not been in contact with the teaching. In common parlance, he has not got the message.

Consider the Buddha's admonition to Vakkali, the devoted bhikkhu who spent all his time in worshipful admiration of the Buddha, "Vakkali, he who does not see the Dhamma does not see me." That is why taking refuge in the Three Gems without empirical knowledge of the Dhamma, i.e. insight into the arising and passing away of phenomena, relies on hearsay only. It is not taking refuge with direct knowledge.

Taking refuge with direct knowledge means imbibing the Buddha's teaching with right view by perceiving the aggregates, the sense bases, and the elements, and their arising and cessation, which alone will destroy the delusion about a "self" and doubts about the Four Noble Truths. This kind of going for refuge is the real refuge, for the worshipper is actually in contact with the Three Gems.

> "One understands suffering, its origin, its cessation and the Noble Eightfold Path leading to the end of suffering. This, indeed, is a secure refuge, this is the supreme refuge. Taking refuge in this, one gains release from the cycle of existences." (Dhp 191-192.)

The above stanzas refer to taking refuge with direct knowledge. As for the seven aspects in the five aggregates discussed earlier, each aspect includes taking refuge based on hearsay and taking refuge with direct knowledge, thus making seven pairs.

Let me illustrate the difference between the two. Suppose there are two lepers at advanced stages of the disease. There is also a competent physician who can cure leprosy. One leper lives a hundred days' journey from the physician. He has never seen the physician, but takes his medicine brought to him by travellers. By taking the medicine faithfully and correctly, eventually he is completely cured of leprosy. The other leper lives in the physician's house as a dependent. He does not take the medicine because he finds its smell and taste unpleasant. He only enjoys the good food that is plentiful at the master's table. The result is obvious; his disease worsens day by day. Of the two lepers, only the one who was cured knows, by direct knowledge, the efficacy of the medicine and the true worth of the physician. The other does not know the real worth of the physician or the medicine he administers. He has only knowledge based on hearsay about the greatness of the physician and the powerful medicine he dispenses. The analogy is clear enough.

So, one who is training to acquire the proficiency in the seven aspects referred to above does not need to utter the words of taking refuge in the Buddha, Dhamma, and Saṅgha. He does not need to go to a pagoda for worship, for these are mere formalities, and not essential, as he or she well understands. It is only for those who fail to practise what the Buddha taught that the utterances and the acts of worship are so important. These "hearsay" worshippers may be Buddhists today, but they may change their religion tomorrow. Those who worship with direct knowledge would rather give up their lives than convert to another religion.

Chapter Eight

The eighth question deals with the fundamentals that govern the case of a non-Buddhist who becomes a Buddhist. What beliefs must one abandon to follow the Buddha's teaching?

The Four Types of Buddhists

One is called a Buddhist if one has the right view about one's volitional actions being one's own real possession that one cannot disown. More specifically, this understanding covers the following ten matters:

1. That giving alms is wholesome kamma.
2. That making offerings is wholesome kamma.
3. That giving even trifling gifts and presents is wholesome kamma.
4. That there are definite and appropriate results from wholesome and unwholesome actions.
5. That there is wholesome kamma in looking after one's mother, and unwholesome kamma in treating her badly.
6. That there is wholesome kamma in looking after one's father, and unwholesome kamma in treating him badly.
7. That there is this human world.
8. That there are also other worlds such as the hell realms and the celestial worlds of devas and brahmās.
9. That there are beings born spontaneously.
10. That there are recluses and brahmins in the world with genuine attainments through right practice, who, having

> realized through direct knowledge the truth regarding this world and the other worlds, make it known to others.

These ten matters are clearly understood by all wise men as within the scope of their mundane knowledge. Such right view, commonly attainable (even without encountering the Buddha or his teaching), is the basic attainment in one who calls himself a Buddhist.

In the world, any wrong view can be dispelled by a knowledge of dependent origination. One is liable to fall into a false view only due to lack of this knowledge. It is vital that Buddhists understand dependent origination and the significance of the factors contained in the discourse on it. One who understands dependent origination may be called a Buddhist of the medium attainments. One who has gained insight into the seven aspects of the five aggregates is a Buddhist of the higher attainments, since this right view is based on insight.

One is a true Buddhist however, only when one has realized the Four Noble Truths. Such a Noble One is a "stream-winner." Why is only a stream-winner called a true Buddhist? It is because taking refuge in the Buddha becomes inseparable from consciousness. In other words, there is no danger of a stream-winner falling into wrong views. Compare this superior attainment with the attainments of the higher or the medium classes, whose absolute confidence in the Three Gems is assured only for the present existence. As for one with only the basic attainment, their faith in the Buddha's teaching cannot be called stable because they might change to another religion tomorrow, if the right circumstances arise.

A stream-winner may be born into a non-Buddhist family but will not be led into professing another religion even on pain of instant death. He or she would rather be burnt alive than forsake his or her firm confidence in the Buddha's teaching. This confidence never falters, but grows until he or she attains nibbāna. That firmness of conviction is referred to by the Buddha as follows:

> "Bhikkhus, there is no possibility for one who has attained right view to indicate another teacher as his or her teacher."

There is another passage that describes a Buddhist:

> "One is a satisfactory Buddhist, if one becomes indignant at being called an adherent of another religion, and is pleased to be called a Buddhist."

In other words, one is pleased to hear the Buddha's teaching extolled and displeased to hear another religion commended.

Chapter Nine

The ninth question asks me to provide a definitive stand that a Buddhist should take when confronted by non-Buddhists, i.e. what are the main aspects of the Buddha's teaching that a Buddhist needs to understand and practise?

The Four Noble Truths Need to be Understood

I have mentioned the main aspects of Buddhism in reply to your fourth question, namely: the five aggregates, the six senses, the elements, dependent origination, the four foundations of mindfulness, etc. These teachings are found only in Buddhism, so a Buddhist worth his salt should be proficient in them.

Other meritorious deeds such as giving, keeping the precepts, meditation for concentration using devices *(kasiṇas)*, meditation on the boundless states of loving-kindness, etc., are usually found in other religions. These teachings or practices are always prevalent in civilized societies. They are universal in the sense that they are practised in all eras, whether or not it is the era of a Buddha. They glorify the civilized world, but they are only mundane. In other world cycles too, such good practices were known. They are practised in universes other than ours. There are human beings and celestial beings in the present world and in innumerable other worlds, where there are also recluses, monks, and brahmins. Gotama the Buddha arose in the world cycle of a hundred-year life-span when the good deeds common even to non-Buddhists were on the wane. In this world cycle,[12] the average person is so polluted with defilements that the Buddha had to dwell at great length on the ordinary deeds of merit.

Only during the time of a Buddha's teaching is there the special advantage of taking refuge in the Three Gems. Only then can giving to the fertile field of the Saṅgha be practised. As for the teaching, it is only when a Buddha's teaching is still extant that the teachings on the aggregates, etc., can be heard. That is why a good Buddhist ought to know them well. The seven aspects referred to earlier, if understood well, make a sound Buddhist.

The firm stand that a Buddhist can take and thus meet any criticism in the present existence is the law of dependent origination. The main knowledge that is the safeguard against any other religion either here or hereafter, until one attains nibbāna, is that of the Four Noble Truths.

Dependent Origination Needs to be Understood

I shall now explain the law of dependent origination. Please commit the twelve links to memory:

> Ignorance *(avijjā)*, mental formations *(saṅkhārā)*, consciousness *(viññāṇa)*, psychophysical phenomena *(nāmarūpa)*, the six senses *(saḷāyatana)*, contact *(phassa)*, feeling *(vedanā)*, craving *(taṇhā)*, attachment *(upādāna)*, becoming *(bhava)*, birth *(jāti)*, aging and death *(jarā-maraṇa)*.

---

12 Classes of world cycle. Human life-spans *(āyukappas)* increase from ten years to an incalculable period *(asaṅkheyya)* and then decrease again to ten years. This period of immense duration is called one intermediate world cycle *(antara kappa)*. A period of sixty-four antara kappas is called one incalculable period *(asaṅkheyya kappa)*. A period of four *asaṅkheyyas* is called one *mahākappa*. "By the word *'kappa'* standing alone *'mahākappa'* is meant." (Childers' Pāli Dictionary on *kappa*) [Translator's Note].

1. Ignorance

Ignorance is the opposite of knowledge. It is synonymous with delusion *(moha)*. The mind is like the sun or the moon; knowledge is like sunlight or moonlight. Ignorance is like an eclipse. When the sun is eclipsed there is no sunlight. When the moon is eclipsed there is no moonlight. Likewise, when the mind is shrouded by ignorance, no knowledge can arise.

Ignorance is also like a cataract that makes the eye opaque and eventually causes blindness. Sensual pleasures aggravate the darkness of delusion in just the same way as a wrong diet or strong, pungent smells aggravate a cataract. Ardent practice for proficiency in the seven aspects is like the medicine that can remove the cataract.

Four Kinds of Ignorance

There are four kinds of ignorance: the ignorance that blinds one to the truth of suffering; the ignorance that blinds one to the truth of the cause of suffering; the ignorance that blinds one to the truth of the cessation of suffering; and the ignorance that blinds one to the truth of the path.

Seven Kinds of Ignorance

The ignorance that blinds one to the first aspect in the five aggregates ... the ignorance that blinds one to the seventh aspect of the five aggregates. Of the five aggregates that constitute a being, the material aggregate is most obvious. In the material aggregate, the element of extension is most obvious. You should first try to distinguish the element of extension within your body. At first, a man blinded by a cataract cannot see even such a bright object as the sun or the moon. Similarly, at first you may not see the earth element, but with sustained effort the darkness shrouding the mind gradually gives way. As the darkness of delusion slowly recedes, the mind regains its ability to see. Remember, delusion is not a total stranger, it is your mind in its negative character. The luminous quality of your mind is the original phenomenon, which, in a normal sensuous environment, is usually dominated by darkness. Light means vision or knowledge—when ignorance has been removed you can see the element of extension in your mind's eye just as plainly as a man with normal eyes can see the sun or the moon.

Having seen the element of extension within your body, proceed to examine the other elements that make up the material aggregate. Having thus understood materiality in its true nature, proceed to understand the four mental aggregates. In this way, the five aggregates will be understood, which means that you are skilful or proficient in the five aggregates, the first aspect. Ignorance has then given way to knowledge. As you rightly discern the remaining six aspects, observe how the light of knowledge dawns on the mind, and how the veil of ignorance is lifted. After the seven kinds of ignorance have been dispelled, and knowledge of the seven aspects is gained, keep up the practice steadfastly to gain the path knowledge that is right view. Once one is established in path knowledge ignorance is absolutely dispelled, and when ignorance disappears the remaining eleven factors of dependent origination also become clear. The Four Noble Truths are then simultaneously realized.

How the Four Noble Truths are Realized

Discerning the truth of suffering *(dukkha sacca)* in the five aggregates, abandoning the ignorance and craving that are the roots of these ills *(samudaya sacca)*, the direct experience of the cessation of the twelve links of dependent origination *(nirodha sacca)*, the arising of insight with path knowledge *(magga sacca)*— all these four realizations occur simultaneously. The three trainings reach maturity, the thirty-seven factors of enlightenment are fulfilled, taking refuge in the Three Gems is well established, and the five māras are vanquished. Māra, the evil deva of the Paranimmitavasavattī realm, the great destroyer and "Tempter," cannot confound such a Noble One. Even if confronted by thousands of non-Buddhist teachers, a Noble One will never be in doubt about the truth.

This is an exposition to underline the crucial importance of ignorance, the principal factor in the law of dependent origination. Although the whole chain of dependent origination is finally broken with the conquest of ignorance, the remaining factors will also be dealt with to understand them more clearly.

2. Mental Formations

All physical, verbal, and mental kammas done with a desire to attain a good life, now and in future existences, are called mental formations. "All kammas" includes the ten moral kammas and the ten immoral kammas. Immoral kammas are committed out of attachment to the present existence, because of ignorance regarding the true nature of the five aggregates. Moral kammas are committed out of desire for future existence, because of ignorance regarding the same five aggregates.

The Buddha and the Arahants, too, perform wholesome actions with even greater diligence than ignorant persons, but having attained path knowledge, they have no attachment to the aggregates that form their existence (which is their last). Therefore, none of their actions, whether physical, verbal, or mental, carry any merit, and are not called saṅkhāras because the necessary volitional activity that clings to present well-being or to future existence is absent. The fact that all mental formations spring from ignorance of the truth is so obvious that even non-Buddhists can probably comprehend it.

3. Consciousness

Consciousness here means rebirth-consciousness, the consciousness that links the previous existence to the present one. The kammic force of previous volitional effort must result in the initial consciousness of the present. How the present existence arises from previous kamma can be known only by supernormal knowledge *(abhiññā)*. It is unfathomable to one of normal intellect. There are certain recluses, monks, and devas who know where a being was before the present existence, but even they do not understand the law that underlies kamma. They think it is due to the transmigration of a soul, and it is exactly on this point that they go wrong. Among the ten aspects of right view, the tenth refers to this supernormal knowledge:

> "There are recluses and brahmins in the world with genuine attainments through right practice, who, having realized through direct knowledge the truth regarding this world and

the other worlds, make it known to others."

Those who lack this right view hold false views on rebirth. Westerners usually lack this right view. Wrong beliefs of various descriptions began to arise in the world aeons ago when monks and recluses who had acquired the *jhānas* and attained supernormal knowledge began to disappear. These wrong beliefs have been spreading since the times when the human life-span was a thousand years, as is said in the *Cakkavattī Sutta* of the *Dīgha Nikāya*.

Nowadays, modern surgeons and scientists, lacking right view, depend on what the eye can see, and putting sole reliance on phenomena visible with the aid of microscopes, propound theories about life and reproduction. Those possessed of right view, however, though the subject is not within their province, do not fall into error because they practise along the right path to understand the subject as well as they can. This is true even outside the Buddha's teaching. When the Buddha arose, they learned the Buddha's teaching and gained right view of a higher order.

> Right view at the elementary level is bound up with personality view. It is only through advanced insight training that personality view can be discarded.

This is a note of warning that rebirth, or rebirth-consciousness, is a really abstruse subject full of pitfalls.

The Relationship of the Aggregates throughout Saṃsāra

The relationship between the material and mental aggregates may be summarized here. Regard the paths of the material and mental aggregates as belonging to separate courses in a given being, each taking its own path of development. In the endless round of rebirths, the material aggregate breaks up on the death of a being, but the mental aggregates never break up until the final passing away of an Arahant (parinibbāna). The material aggregate has no sense-faculties, nor can it think about or comprehend things, which are the functions of the mental aggregates. The mental aggregates do not have any form or substance, not even the tiniest atom, which is the property of the material aggregate.

The Course of the Material Aggregate

Let us see the course that the material aggregate takes. We shall consider two cases, the flow of a river and the path of a storm.

The waters of a river, in flowing from its source to the great ocean, comprise the primary elements of heat and motion. The water undergoes constant changes in temperature. The cold in the previous material element of the water causes the element of cold to arise; the heat in the previous material element causes the material element of heat to arise. The element of cohesion has the property of weight so that it causes the water level to go down the gradient. The primary element of motion is constantly pushing away the material elements of the water as the fresh cold or hot material elements arise. These can arise only at some distance (not visible to the physical eye) from the parent material qualities. Being subject to the element of cohesion, the new material elements can arise only at some lower level. This is what we call the flow of the waters in a river (which is in reality the material aggregate with its constituent four primary elements taking their own course under a given set of circumstances).

Now consider a storm. The element of cohesion is not the dominant force as with the river. The element of cohesion only has the power of holding the material phenomena together. Since the storm is not being weighed down like the river water, it does not flow downwards. The element of motion is dominant here. So whether occurring over the ocean or on the land, the motive force can push it at great speeds over the vast area where it occurs. The fresh material phenomena that arise take place only at a certain distance from the parent material phenomena, they do not break away from the old. The new arises only dependent upon the old.

The same principle of fresh material phenomena arising at some distance from the old material phenomena applies with lightning. Here the distance between fresh material phenomena, i.e. the flash of lightning from the sky above and the earth below, is much greater than that in a storm or in a river's current. It all depends on the constituent element of motion: the stronger the element, the greater the distance. This is the way that the material aggregate occurs.

The Course of the Mental Aggregates

When the mental aggregates arise dependent upon the material aggregate, they do not occur apart from it. Since they do not break up, their occurrence cannot take place away from the material aggregate until the moment when the latter breaks up (at the death of a given being). Among the mental aggregates, volition plays the key role, not unlike the element of heat in the material aggregate. From the viewpoint of conditional relations, it is called "kamma-relation." Beliefs such as wrong and right view and the other mental properties are comparable to the primary element of motion in the material aggregate. This is called "the relationship of means" *(magga paccaya)*. Each existence is the result of a volition that has a given effect. The element of heat, for example, has its effects on the proximate material phenomena in a series. This effect can last only as long as the five aggregates of a being last. As for volition, once the resultant consciousness has arisen, its effects can occur for innumerable existences. However, the kammic force may remain dormant for innumerable world cycles until favourable conditions occur. The results of one's kamma remain as potential both in the mental aggregates and in the material aggregate.[13] Technically these kammas form the "residual" type of kamma or *kaṭattā-kamma*. It therefore follows that the continuity of mental aggregates is uninterrupted. So one can say, conventionally speaking, that "the same" mental aggregates prevail, though hundreds of thousands of world cycles may pass.

This is a fundamental difference between the material and mental aggregates. No parallel exists in the material aggregate. Only the roughest comparison can be made. Even in the present existence the two are noticeably different. Try to observe this within yourself.

At the breaking up of the existing material aggregate, the mental aggregates take rebirth with a fresh material aggregate elsewhere. How far away from the old body can consciousness take its rebirth? It depends on the volition (comparable to the

---

13 *Kaṭattā rūpānaṃ:* when the residual kamma ripens, co-existent material phenomena at rebirth are due to deeds done in a former birth (*kaṭattā* = having been done.) [Though the fruits of a tree are not literally "stored" in the tree, the tree is a potential source of fruits in due season (ed.)]

element of heat) and the other mental concomitants such as right or wrong views, which are comparable to the functioning of motion (i.e. the relation of means). The text calls them "the mental formations that have the power of casting out *(khipanaka saṅkhārānaṃ)*." When the relation of means is strong enough, rebirth-consciousness may arise in the highest brahmā realm called *nevasaññā-nāsaññā*. At the other extreme, it may arise in the deepest hell (*Avīci*). Consciousness of the mind-base can apprehend things unhindered by any physical barrier. Mental phenomena are therefore incomparably more powerful than material phenomena.

Being ignorant of the power of mental phenomena, modern thinkers reason based on the material phenomena that they can observe, and deduce theories of life based on such observations. All these theories are nothing but futile exercises in wrong thinking. This is impressed upon you because rebirth-consciousness offers a ready ground for confrontation by other religions. When one discusses Buddhism with others, one ought to be sure of what one is saying. One should speak out of conviction acquired by direct knowledge. Reliance on shallow knowledge or texts learnt by rote will only bring discredit to Buddhism.

4. Psychophysical Phenomena

By *nāma* the three mental aggregates of feeling, perception, and mental formations are meant, which are mental concomitants. The mental aggregate of consciousness is supreme in the ultimate sense. Its supremacy has been mentioned earlier (p.50). It is the leader *(jeṭṭha)*, the chief *(seṭṭha)*, pre-eminent *(padhāna)*, the principal *(pamukha)* without which no mental phenomena can exist, the lord *(rāja)* of all the six senses.

How Body and Mind Arise

When a person is reborn in Tāvatiṃsa due to the acquisition of powerful merits, the celestial mansion for a deva of that realm is at once present. By the same analogy, whenever consciousness arises, feeling, perception, contact, volition, etc., arise simultaneously. The body including the four elements also arises. Since rebirth-consciousness is the dominant factor in the process, it is said that body and mind have consciousness as their origin. In the case of rebirth in the womb, the initial arising of material phenomena is invisible to the naked eye. Just as a tiny seed of the banyan tree grows into a magnificent tree, from the moment of conception an embryo develops gradually into a living being (such as human being, etc.) as follows:

1. In the first seven days, as embryonic liquid (invisible at first);
2. In the second seven days, as a foamy substance;
3. In the third seven days, as a clot of blood;
4. In the fourth seven days, as a tiny lump of flesh.

Then at the end of the eleventh week, the head and limbs take shape when the four sense bases of eye, ear, nose, and tongue are formed. The two sense bases of body and mind arise at conception. This is (roughly) how materiality arises.

Scientific knowledge is limited primarily to what the microscope can reveal. It is therefore beyond the ability of modern scientists to observe the subtle material phenomena. Based on physiological findings alone, they can only define animal and human faculties.

5. The Six Senses

The six senses—the eye, ear, nose, tongue, body, and mind—are called *saḷāyatana*. The first five are included in the material aggregate. The sixth, the mind, is nothing but consciousness. Although the six senses are included in psychophysical phenomena, they are repeated as the fifth link of dependent origination due to their importance. They are the six main doors in a being like the main gates of a city. They may also be called the six head offices, the six warehouses, the six ports, or the six railway terminals.

It is through these six ports that the six kinds of steamships travel to the various destinations—the heavenly realms or the realms of misery. Similarly, it is through these six railway terminals that the six trains set out on their journeys in saṃsāra.

The Buddha said, "What, monks, is the arising of the world? Because of the eye and visible object, eye-consciousness arises. The meeting of the three—the eye, the visible object, and eye-consciousness—is contact. Because of contact, feeling arises. Because of feeling ... Thus arises this whole mass of suffering. This, monks, is called the arising of the world."

In the above discourse, the Buddha expounds how the six senses condition the aggregates and their attendant suffering. If the inhabitants of hell were grouped according to their mode of descent, there would be six groups as follows:

1. Those who travelled there by the eye-base;
2. Those who travelled there by the ear-base;
3. Those who travelled there by the nose-base;
4. Those who travelled there by the tongue-base;
5. Those who travelled there by the body-base;
6. Those who travelled there by the mind-base.

To extend the metaphor: they travelled from those six main terminals, or they set out from those six ports.

The arising of the mental aggregates is quite different from that of the material aggregate. As for the material aggregate, a tiny seedling from a banyan tree can grow into a big tree, and from the seeds produced by that tree during its lifetime, thousands of banyan trees can be propagated. As for the mental aggregate of mental formations, each kamma produces only one existence at a time. Even within one sitting, six volitions can arise out of the six senses, all of which will produce a result sometime if not during one's present lifetime. In the next existence, too, since only one of them is going to give its fruit, the rest are delayed until favourable opportunities prevail. They may be likened to trains standing in a station with their engines running, waiting for a green light. That green light may take aeons to appear, but eventually it will appear, as will the result of mental formations unless one becomes a stream-winner. As for a blind worldling submerged in immorality, trains to carry him or her to the hell realms are being made ready every day.

How is one destined for such miserable existences? It depends upon the stimulation of the sense bases. Take the eye-base for instance. Some enticing form that belongs to someone else appears to view, and the eye-base contacts it, so eye-consciousness arises. It is like the spark that occurs when the hammer strikes the flint in a cigarette lighter. Due to the presence of three factors—visible object, the eye, and eye-consciousness—contact arises. Contact is like the hand that grasps the visible object. The moment it grasps it, feeling arises. Here, feeling is like a withered lotus coming into contact with cool water. Feeling is enjoyed as pleasant. This causes craving or attachment to arise. Attachment does not let go of that pleasant feeling. No craving arises in the Buddha and the Arahants, although they know that a thing can evoke pleasure, since they see the danger of being attached to pleasant feeling.

For example, when an unwary person finds a poisonous fruit which looks like the choicest mango, and smells and tastes like it too, he will be enticed by the appearance, smell, and taste. However, someone who knows that the fruit is poisonous, far from being enticed, will laugh at it and scorn it in fear. This is how, on seeing some desirable thing, different reactions arise in one who has defilements and one who is free from defilements.

Pleasant feeling or attachment may be likened to the sticky substance used by hunters to trap monkeys. When one is pleased with the object, craving for the pleasant feeling grows, intensifies, and becomes rooted in the sense object. The roots extend deeper and take a firm hold like the roots of a banyan tree clinging to and creeping into decaying brickwork. (How this process of attachment arises will be dealt with later.) The attachment that arises from craving is called "sensual attachment" *(kāmupādāna)*.

Attachment arises immediately in one who is in the habit of falling into lust. If the object of attachment is one's own property, it holds him fast to the round of existences but does not pull him down to hell. If the object of attachment is the property of another, and one does not covet it, the attachment may not send one down to the hell realms. When, however, one covets another's property, this attachment is unwholesome kamma. Scheming to take another's property is an evil volition that amounts to a mental act of covetousness *(abhijjhā)*. It has the potential to push one down to hell. It, too, is like a train that will carry one to the realms of torture.

Further, if one bears malice against the owner of the property that one covets, it is the evil volition of ill-will *(vyāpāda)*. This also has the potential to send one down to hell. Again, if one believes that harbouring malice is not a serious evil, and that those recluses and wise men who say it is are wrong; that there is no such thing as kamma; that malicious thoughts produce no result; that the worse that could happen is that anger would arise in the owner if he comes to know of the ill-will directed against him—that amounts to the evil volition of wrong view. This is another train to take one down to hell. Beginning from feasting one's eyes on another's property, a string of other immoral deeds may also be perpetrated, such as killing, stealing, adultery, lying, backbiting, abusive speech, gossiping, or idle chatter—all of which provide sure transport to the realms of torture. These immoral volitions that cause one to commit the ten immoral deeds are what is meant by: "Because of attachment, becoming arises."

This is how, from the eye-base alone, one of the six "railway terminals," trains depart daily for the fiery realms bearing the unwary, ignorant people. The same should be understood in respect of the other five bases and the other five terminals.

It is from the very same terminals that the six trains to the fortunate planes of existence depart. Herein, since I am confining myself to using everyday examples only, the more abstruse matters regarding the consequences that birth entails are not touched upon. From such sense bases (terminals in our example), ten trains leave for the four lower planes of existence due to the ten immoral actions. Ten trains leave for the fortunate planes of existence due to the ten moral actions. The fortunate realms are the human, deva, and brahmā planes. This is why the six senses are taught as a separate factor though they are already included in consciousness and psychophysical phenomena.

6–8. Contact, Feeling, and Craving

These factors have already been examined in our discussion on how the ten moral and immoral deeds are based at the six senses using the analogy of the six trains.

9. Attachment

The significance of attachment *(upādāna)* will now be explained. To one who fails to understand things in their true nature, the twelve factors of dependent origination seem inadequate to describe life. It is said, by the poet, "The world is too much with us." However, in truth, one has to see the world only in the light of these twelve factors. Failure to do so allows a persistent state of craving to prevail that naturally inclines one to harbour wrong views and personality view.

All the existences of beings in the human world, or the higher worlds of the devas and the brahmās, or the lower worlds of the four realms of misery, arise due to the causal factors of consciousness and psychophysical phenomena. This fact must be understood. These two factors bring about what is tangible.

The six senses, contact, and feeling are the three factors that manipulate and adorn the tangible bodies of beings. Craving and attachment are the bold banners of the ordinary person signifying the manipulation and adornment (by the three manipulators) on the body. Regarding the banner of attachment there are four kinds:

i. Sensual attachment *(kāmupādāna)*;
ii. Attachment to wrong view *(diṭṭhupādāna)*;
iii. Attachment to futile practices or rituals *(sīlabbatupādāna)*;
iv. Attachment to personality view *(attāvādupādāna)*.

i. *Kāmupadāna* means tenacious attachment to magnificent existence as a man, deva, or Sakka, the celestial lord of the Tāvatiṃsa realm, just as the roots of the banyan tree cling to the crevices in brickwork. It is, in essence, craving. It is comparable to Balavamukha—the awesome whirlpool in the great oceans, the dread of all seafarers. If sucked into the whirlpool of sensual attachment, one is dragged down directly to hell. Most beings are spun around by the powerful whirlpool of sensuality so that even when a Buddha arises in the world, they miss the rare opportunity to comprehend the Dhamma because they cling to existence so desperately. They cannot hear the teaching even now, though it is still loud and clear.

Craving, which takes pleasure in the six senses and their objects, may be likened to the peripheral currents of the great whirlpool, from which one could, with mindful determination, extricate oneself, However, if one advances too far into the currents, the whirlpool will drag one down. All seafarers, once caught in it, are sucked down into the ocean's depths. Similarly, once attachment has established itself in one's mind, one is inextricably drawn into the saṃsāric current and cast down to the depths of hell.

ii. *Diṭṭhupādāna* means the sixty-two confirmed wrong views[14] and the three gross wrong views *(visamahetu diṭṭhi)*.[15]

iii. *Sīlabbatupādāna* means futile practices and rites held to with religious fervour. An example of the worst type is to believe that if one models one's life on that of an ox or a dog one attains eternal bliss.

iv. *Attavādupādāna* is personality view, attachment to a sense of "self," which we have discussed earlier.

10. Becoming

Becoming is understood as a process of kamma as the active side *(kammabhava)*, which determines the passive side *(upapattibhava)* of the next existence. The ten moral kammas and the ten immoral kammas are the active side. Moral kammas result in fortunate existences as a wealthy human, deva, or brahmā. Immoral kammas result in rebirth in the four lower realms: the hell realm, the animal realm, hungry ghosts *(petas)*, and fallen gods *(asurakāyas)*. These existences, both high and low, are the passive side of existence *(upapattibhava)*.

11–12. Birth, Aging, and Death

Birth means rebirth or continued existences in the future, as a new set of the five aggregates.

Aging means the constant decay of phenomena manifested as senility. After arising, the five aggregates decay and perish incessantly. Decay is called aging; perishing is called death.

---

14 The sixty-two kinds of wrong views *(micchā-diṭṭhi)* include eighteen kinds relating to the past and forty-four relating to the future. All are based on personality view. Again, seven views hold that the soul is annihilated after death *(uccheda-diṭṭhi)* and fifty-five hold that the soul is eternal *(sassata-diṭṭhi)*. See the *Brahmajāla Sutta, Dīgha Nikāya*.

15 (i) The belief that all is the result of previous kamma *(pubbekatahetu-diṭṭhi)*, (ii) the belief that all is due to the will of Almighty God *(issaranimmānahetu-diṭṭhi)*, (iii) the belief that all is without any cause *(akiriyahetu-diṭṭhi)*. They are gross because they either disregard or distort the principle of kamma. See *Sammādiṭṭhi Dīpanī* by Ledi Sayādaw in *Manuals of Buddhism*, Rangoon 1981.

Some Difficult Points in Dependent Origination

The first two factors—ignorance and mental formations—are the past causes that lie at the root of the present existence. In other words, our previous deluded actions have "created" our present existence. Who creates all beings? Ignorance and mental formations create them all. There is no other Creator. (Ignorance and mental formations have already been explained above.)

What happens after death? Rebirth follows death. Rebirth is a fresh becoming. The eight intermediate factors from *viññāṇa* to *bhava* belong to the present. That is what is generally called "life" or "the world." The cycle of rebirth is without beginning. In that beginningless cycle, when you consider the present existence, it is just a manifestation of your previous ignorance and mental formations. As soon as the present life ceases, a fresh rebirth arises. That fresh birth is also another "present" existence. In other words, one existence after another is arising, so there is always a "present" existence as long as ignorance and craving remain. This is the eternal cycle of existence called saṃsāra.

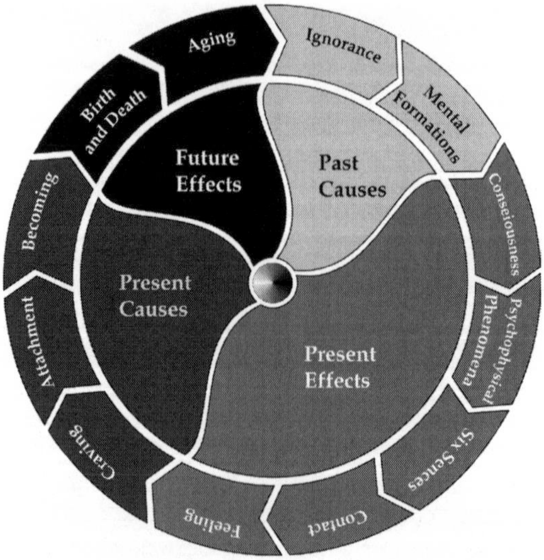

The Buddha taught about ignorance and mental formations to show that there is no other Creator. He taught about birth to show that as long as craving and attachment are present, there is no end to the round of births.

Ignorance and mental formations cannot arise by themselves. They can arise only when the eight factors such as consciousness are present. So whenever there are ignorance and mental formations, the eight factors must be in existence. The eight also are only a creation of the previous ignorance and mental formations. Thus the beginning of saṃsāra cannot be known. This shows that it is a mistake to think that there must be a first cause of a being. It also does away with another wrong view—the theory of transmigration of a soul, i.e. that the same being is reborn after death. A fresh birth must always arise if craving and attachment are present. By birth is meant the eight factors such as consciousness that are present right now—generally called the present birth or the present life.

The round of births therefore ends only when craving and attachment are extinguished. Otherwise there is no end to existence on some plane or another. Craving and attachment do not die out unless one contemplates thoroughly on the seven aspects in the five aggregates. It is only when right view is attained through insight that craving ceases. When craving is extinct, attachment is automatically dead and gone.

The Buddha taught a way that an ordinary person can follow. How does seawater taste? If one tastes a drop of seawater at the seashore, one knows that it is salty. One need not taste water from the middle of all the great oceans to know this. In much the same way, the Buddha explains how the eight factors of dependent origination arise through previous ignorance and mental formations. This shows that dependent origination and the eight factors are knowable. It is enough to understand their past arising. To ask when previous ignorance began is as futile as tasting water from all the great oceans to know whether seawater is salty. The previous ignorance and mental formations arose just because there were those eight factors present in a previous existence. So to trace back all the previous existences would be an endless search. More importantly, it serves no purpose and is not conducive to attaining nibbāna. This is the reason for saying that saṃsāra is without any beginning.

The Dangers of Aging and Death

In all the realms of existence, aging and death are the real dangers. All animate or inanimate things that one thinks one possesses (including the body and the mind) contain the elements of aging and death. Therefore, one is subject to the dangers of fire, water, disease, poisonous or ferocious animals, evil spirits, and so on. One who has epilepsy is in constant danger of having a fit on hearing exciting music. Similarly, the constant danger of aging and death is inherent in all beings. Life-spans are spoken of because death is a sure thing. So we say, for instance, that the Cātumaharājikā devaloka has a five-hundred year life-span or that the Tāvatiṃsa devaloka has a thousand-year life-span, etc.

It is due to the element of aging and death that we have to busy ourselves with the daily chores of maintaining our existence, or on a spiritual level, with onerous meritorious deeds such as giving, virtue, training and cultivating the mind, and so on.

In all the planes of existence, aging and death are the only real dangers. They are the only fires in the ultimate sense. All the activities of each living being are undertaken just to serve the fires of aging and death. Every existence ends in decay and death. (A proper presentation of this point should convince any non-Buddhist of these facts.)

Q. Where do aging and death originate?
A. They originate in birth.

Birth implies decay and death. Where there is no birth, decay and death cannot arise. This is a plain fact with which non-Buddhists can readily agree. However, one needs to understand birth in its ultimate sense. The arising of any sensation within us, where it arises, how it feels, what sort of illness it is, what sort of pain, etc., are "births," as are the varying frames of mind or mental feelings.

Q. Where does rebirth originate?
A. It originates in becoming, both wholesome and unwholesome.

No rebirth can arise unless there is the potential of one's previous deeds to be realized. There is no Creator who creates life other than one's own kammic force. This point is profound. It is no easy matter to explain to the satisfaction of all. Even among traditional Buddhists, whatever right view they have is only shallow—direct insight into the elements and phenomena is still lacking. So the way in which the material and mental aggregates function should be clearly understood.

The question of birth is the one over which one is most likely to fall into wrong views if one happens to live outside Buddhist tradition and culture. That is why it is crucial to have the right view regarding who can show the truth, having himself known it through training and insight, the tenth subject in the ten aspects of mundane right view (see p.96).

Q. Where does becoming originate?
A. It originates in attachment.
Q. Where does attachment originate?
A. It originates in craving.
Q. Where does craving originate?
A. It arises from feeling. These points should be clear to non-Buddhists as well.
Q. How do pleasant and unpleasant feelings arise?
A. They arise due to contact. This point will not be readily acceptable to non-Buddhists.

It is a controversial question for them. Even among Buddhists, some wrong beliefs can arise on this point. For there are many so-called Buddhists who believe that all internal and external feelings, pleasant or unpleasant, are due to previous kamma alone. "It is as fate (*kamma*) would have it," they would say, or "If luck is with us we may have something to eat," or "It is bad kamma that caused this misfortune," or "It is through good kamma alone that one prospers," and so on. Such exclusive dependence upon the power and effect of past kamma is not correct. It is a form of wrong view called *"pubbekatahetu-diṭṭhi"* or the belief that all is conditioned by past kamma. This is according to the Suttas and also the Abhidhamma.

Kamma is like seed-grain. Joy or sorrow (pleasant or unpleasant feeling) are like the paddy, making an effort is like the fertility of the soil, knowledge or skill are like the rain or irrigation water. The same seed-grain yields a good or poor crop depending upon the fertility of the soil, the supply of water, and most of all, effort exerted at the right time and in the right way. Indeed kamma is highly dependent on present effort. The seed-grain is no more significant than good soil and regular watering of a paddy field. Even the best of seeds, such as the Abbhantara[16] fruit's stone, will not thrive in poor soil and in dry conditions. A successful birth can result only when proper prenatal care is given and arrangements have been made for the birth. Again, present results also depend on skill, discretion, and prompt effort.

Some people lack knowledge and skill besides effort. They fall on hard times, too. No wonder, then, that they become poor. They blame fate or previous kamma. They would point to the exceptional cases of those lucky ones who prosper without skill or effort. In fact their knowledge about kamma is scanty and shallow.

Because one's previous kamma has been deficient in wholesome deeds, one may be born ugly, physically deformed, or handicapped. Such congenital deficiencies are the result of past kamma, which one can do very little to alter. Once one has been born, the matter of upbringing, personal care, working for a living, acquiring wealth and merits, etc., are up to oneself. This is present kamma, which depends primarily on one's own wisdom and effort. One's progress in the world depends very much on present kamma.

Although kamma is related to pleasure and pain, it is not the cause of feeling. As the Buddha said, "Because of contact, feeling arises." He did not say, "Because of kamma, feeling arises." Certain other religions do not recognize kamma, which is one extreme of wrong view. However, some Buddhists place all their faith in kamma to the exclusion of effort and prudence. This is the other extreme of wrong view called "*pubbekatahetu-diṭṭhi*." Those who hold the latter wrong view maintain:

16 The legendary mango of divine taste, a very rare fruit said to grow in the heart of the Himalayan mountains (*Abbhantara* = interior).

"Whatever pleasant, unpleasant, or neutral feeling one experiences is due to a previous cause."

When a banyan tree seed is planted, its successful sprouting depends on the soil, water supply, and seed-grain. Of these three, the seed-grain is most vital; the soil and moisture are only supporting factors. Once germination has taken place, the growth of the tree depends on the soil and moisture only, for the seed-grain has discharged its function, and is no longer needed. This is a practical example. The potential inherent in the genes of the seed determines the size of the tree and its longevity, but this potential can only be realized with the help of soil and water. Only when this help is available can the potential in the seed be realized to the full. Here, the difference in the species of seeds must be understood. A tree's size and longevity depend on its species. It is the same for grasses and other types of vegetation. In this example, the seed-grain is like kamma, the tree like our body, the soil like our due efforts, and water like prudence.

The kamma that one has accumulated from the beginningless past is a unique mixture of good and bad. Skilful effort and prudence will be the dominant factors contributing to progress. One is doing oneself a disservice if one blames kamma for one's failures in life; so too if one blames the lack of perfections for failing to acquire learning, merit, and insight in one's religious life. Ponder on this well.

"From contact, feeling arises": It is cold in winter, and cold is unpleasant. Certain teachers maintain that it is cold because God has willed the seasons. This is a kind of wrong view called "*issaranimmāna-diṭṭhi*." Those who believe this maintain:

"Whatever pleasant, unpleasant, or neutral feeling one experiences is due to an Almighty God."

Certain teachers hold that there is no cause or condition for what a person experiences. Those who believe this maintain:

"Whatever pleasant, unpleasant, or neutral feeling one experiences is without cause."

Certain naked ascetics taught that pleasure and pain are the result of past kamma and nothing else. This is also a wrong view called "*pubbekatahetu-diṭṭhi.*" This view is partly true, but it is still a wrong view because it rules out causes and conditions other than kamma.

The law of dependent origination says:

> "Body consciousness arises dependent on the body and a tactile object. The coincidence of the three is contact, and feeling is conditioned by contact."

Cold is felt in the following way according to the Buddha's teaching quoted above. There is the body-base inside you. There is the material element of heat, which can become cold (a quality of the heat element). This serves as the sense object, the tangible kind that corresponds to the sensitive body-base. As the sense object (cold) and the sense base (body) come into contact, tactile-consciousness arises throughout the body. These three elements of cold, body-base, and tactile-consciousness condition the mental factor called contact. This contact causes feeling to arise. Here, it is the unpleasant feeling of cold, and one might say, "Oh, it's terribly cold." When one approaches a fire, the cold feeling vanishes, and a pleasant feeling of warmth arises in its place. How does this new feeling come about? Is it God's will? Or is it purely a matter of kamma?

Similarly, when the external material quality of warmth contacts the sensitive body-base, tactile-consciousness arises. Consciousness arises dependent on the body, so it is called tactile-consciousness. This, in turn, causes feeling born of body-contact *(kāya-samphassajā-vedanā)* to arise. The vanishing of the external cold material quality leads to the vanishing of the tactile-consciousness and of the cold feeling thus produced. When one moves away from the fireplace, the pleasant feeling of warmth vanishes. The same causal law should be applied here too.

By the same principle, when one feels hot and sweaty in summer one takes a cool shower. The arising of the pleasant cool feeling should be understood in the same way. These examples illustrate the arising of contact in the sensitive body-base and the consequent arising of pleasant or unpleasant feelings. Feelings arising through the other five sense bases should be understood in the same way.

The causal law is universally applicable. In our illustration, the change from unpleasant to pleasant feeling is caused by one's effort, which is merely present action, though, to a certain extent, it is assignable to kamma. However, such a view cannot help to dispel personality view and doubt. It is only when contact is understood as the dependent factor on which feeling arises, that the vague belief in a "self" and doubts about the Four Noble Truths will be dispelled. Otherwise, the fires of hell burn relentlessly within. Previous kamma, of course, has its role here, but it is just a remote cause like the seed that has grown into a tree. What is most obvious is that the world is a thick forest of desirable and undesirable sense objects. Since the six sense doors are always open, how could any individual prevent pleasant and unpleasant feelings or sensations arising?

Present activities may be motivated by greed, anger, or delusion; or they may be inspired by confidence and knowledge. They include meritorious deeds such as giving or virtue, which may be for one's own benefit or for the benefit of others. None of them are the effects of previous kamma; they result from present effort and present undertakings only. From one's own efforts, one experiences all sorts of feelings. Whether doing a moral deed or an immoral deed, when the necessary conditions prevail, an appropriate contact arises, and dependent on that particular contact, feeling must arise.

This question of pleasant or unpleasant feelings and how they originate is a thorny problem that troubles followers of other religions. Even during the Buddha's time, wrong views on this question were prevalent. That is why it has been given such comprehensive treatment.

The Four Noble Truths Explained

Everyone normally seeks safety, and strives for well-being. All mundane activities are aimed at avoiding discomfort and enjoying pleasure in some way or other. No one wants to get into trouble. No one knowingly tries to hurt himself. Everyone wants to enjoy pleasure and is striving towards that end. Although everyone wants pleasure and happiness and fears pain and sorrow, few know what really ails the world, or what real happiness is.

The Real Ill is Aging and Death

The main ill in the world is aging and death. The danger of death and how it destroys all existences has already been discussed at length and illustrated by the examples of the fire-worshippers and the spendthrift wife. Aging paves the way for death. So whatever illustrations we have used concerning death also apply to aging.

Wherever an ordinary person is born, two hell fires are burning within. One is personality view and the other is doubt (about the Four Noble Truths). Aging and death are the agents in the service of the two fires. They destroy one who is attached to existence, as all beings are. When they have completed their mission of destruction and a being breaks up into the constituent aggregates, the two fires of personality view and doubt cast that being down into hell. They can seize this opportunity only at the breaking up of the five aggregates. The two fires burn within all individuals, even if they are born in one of the six deva realms or in the brahmā realms.

The Buddha said, "Through not understanding this law of dependent origination, Ānanda, these beings are all confused in their existences, like a spoilt skein, or like a weaver bird's nest, or like dried *muñja* grass. They cannot escape from falling into the realms of misery, all in disarray."

The Danger of Falling in Disarray

If you ask someone, "Where will you be born after death?" the reply will probably be, "I don't know; it depends on my kamma."

That is true. Nobody can aim at a certain future existence: it depends on one's kamma. All have to resign themselves to their own kamma. It is just like withered leaves scattered in a strong wind—no one knows where they are going to fall. Not only are human beings subject to an uncertain destination after death, but so too are the devas and brahmās, up to the Vehapphala Brahmā realm. All ordinary persons are in the same situation. They fall in disarray, quite unprepared, to wherever their kamma sends them at their death. Individuals who have passed away from the four formless brahmā realms share the same fate. According to the Nakhasikhā Sutta (S II 263.) most of them fall into the four realms of misery.

Let us give an illustration. Suppose there is a magnificent multi-storeyed mansion. On the first storey, there are plenty of pleasures and the life-span is one month. The second storey provides even more pleasures, and the life-span is two months. As we go up the levels, the pleasures on offer are greater and the life-spans longer. Below the great mansion are areas of scrub land full of thorns and sharp-edged rocks. There are enormous holes filled with sewage and excrement. There are wide areas where sharp spikes are standing. Deep crevices and hollows filled with burning coals lie at the bottom of this place. None falling there could have any chance of escape.

Around the great mansion prevailing winds blow at every storey. The inhabitants of the first storey are swept away by the prevailing winds at the end of their one month life-span. Many of them fall onto the thorny scrub land, many fall into the sewage-filled holes, many drop helplessly onto the standing spikes, many fall down to the fiery hollows. The inhabitants of the upper storeys of the grand mansion share the same fate at the end of their life-span.

The analogy is this: the multi-storeyed mansion is like the human, deva, and brahmā worlds. The terrible terrain below is like the four realms of misery, the prevailing winds like aging and death.

During life one is obsessed with enjoying whatever pleasures one can gain, quite heedless of death; but when death comes, one loses one's bearings. Through attachment to the notion of a self, one is cast down by kamma and falls in disarray. The same thing happens in the deva and brahmā realms as well, and this has been happening since the dawn of time. This complete helplessness at death, when one's kamma usually casts one down into the four realms of misery, is called "*vinipāta*." This is the law of kamma that governs all ordinary persons.

This danger besets the multitude. Its danger and relentlessness during one's lifetime should be understood from the analogies of the fire-worshipper and the spendthrift wife. Aging and death not only destroy, but they also send one to hell because of one's attachment to personality view. All beings are subject to the misfortunes of decay and death, and all have the fires of hell burning within them. That is why all existences are simply dreadful—*dukkha*.

The Present Dangers of Decay and Death

I shall now explain the evils of decay and death to which one is subject during one's lifetime. Since one's birth there has not been a single moment, not so much as a single breath, when one was free from the danger of death. Death is lurking from the time a being is born, and it has always been like this. Mortality keeps beings in constant danger, for there are any number of ways to die. For instance, food is not normally poisonous. However, food can cause an allergic reaction. Though you choose some delicacy to pamper your palate, on eating it you may suddenly become ill and die. Death has countless ways to fulfil its mission. Why should good food turn deadly? Why should this happen to anyone? It is simply because there is a disease in beings (aging, in the ultimate sense) that is always faithfully aiding death. This is just one example of how death can overtake us at any moment. If there was no danger of death, one need not fear anything, not even a thunderbolt striking one's head.

All human endeavours such as earning a livelihood, living in organized society, maintaining law and order, protecting oneself, one's property, etc., are primarily aimed at self-preservation. This, in simple terms, is an attempt to ward off the dangers of death. The danger of death is also a motivating factor in doing meritorious deeds such as giving or virtue. The religious life is also taken up because of an awareness of death's peril. This is an explanation of the dangers of aging and death during one's lifetime.

Of all the ills to which people are subject, aging and death are paramount. There is nothing in the world, whether human or celestial, animate or inanimate, that is free from these two agents of destruction. All material or mental phenomena are fraught with aging and death. Knowing this, one may have done innumerable acts of merit in innumerable previous existences as good humans, devas, or brahmās, all aimed at escaping the fate of falling in disarray. Yet nothing now remains to protect one from such an ignoble fate. One is still just as vulnerable as ever. Those existences have come and gone. The present existence is a fresh aggregate of the same type of suffering. What a waste! One has to start from scratch again. Why have all your good works come to naught? It is because you do not yet know what dukkha is. You have been serving the fires of dukkha in doing good deeds hoping to escape from suffering. So you have taken the trouble to perform the meritorious deeds such as giving, virtue, mental development and training, diligence, concentration, insight, acquiring skills repeatedly throughout saṃsāra. Your present efforts and meritorious undertakings can also become the fuel that feeds the fires of dukkha whose competent helpers are the decay, aging, and death within you. This exhortation is to illustrate the destructive nature of dukkha.

Real Happiness

Real happiness is the freedom from the dangers of aging and death. I shall make this clear. The highest form of human happiness is to be a Universal Monarch *(Cakkavattī)*, but the fires of aging and death burn in him too, as in any other being. He is also enslaved by personality view, and is prone to doubts about the Four Noble Truths. These fires are manifested as life-spans. When aging burns up a human existence in ten years, it is said that ten years is the life-span of man. Understand it in the same way for all life-spans. Life-spans in the deva and brahmā realms are of the same nature. When the human life-span lasts a hundred years a man's youth is burnt up in thirty-three years; his middle age in another thirty-three years and his old age in the last thirty-three years. Or if the length of a human's life is just thirty years, the first decade is consumed by aging in just ten years, the second in the next ten years, and so on.

In the three seasons of the year, the material elements that have existed in the cold season are burnt up in four months; those of the rainy season, in four months; and those of the hot season, in four months, respectively. Of the twelve months in a year, the material elements of the first month are burnt up in thirty days; those of the second month, in thirty days; and so on. Contemplate on the burning of aging in you, in the same way, down to the shortest time span you can imagine, down to the blinking of an eye.

From the most fleeting moment to world cycles or aeons, aging is at work without interruption. Underlying it is the ultimate destroyer—death, a more terrifying fire. Aging or decay is very powerful, so you need to understand it. Unless you can perceive decay at work, you have not gained a clear perception of the causal process. You must be able to pinpoint the "culprit" of the whole scheme. So much for aging or decay. As for death and personality view, I have already explained them above.

Vicikicchā or doubt is a close associate of ignorance or delusion. Doubt is of two kinds: doubt relating to the Dhamma and doubt relating to the soul or self.

The first kind of doubt springs from the ignorance that misconceives things such as the aggregates, sense bases, and elements making up a being. A traveller in unfamiliar terrain, having lost his bearings, thinks that the right way is wrong. He is confused and cannot decide which is the right way. Likewise, due to ignorance, one does not know the earth as the earth element. Doubt makes one vacillate concerning the truth, it also dampens one's fervour to continue in the search for truth. This is doubt about the Dhamma.

The second kind of doubt arises from attachment to the notion of a vague "self" or "soul." One unskilled in dependent origination is upset when faced with death. One is shocked at the prospect of losing the present life, which one believes is one's own. One who holds wrong views dreads that after death his or her "self" may be lost for ever. One who holds right view (mundane right view only) fears falling into one of the four lower realms. That feeling arises from remorse for immoral deeds or having neglected to do meritorious deeds, or both. It is this feeling that magnifies the fear of death at the last, helpless moment. All this vexation and uncertainty about the future casts beings down into the four realms of misery after death.

Personality view and doubt oppress a person on his or her deathbed like a mountain tumbling down. The danger of falling in disarray worries the Universal Monarch as it does other individuals. Even a Universal Monarch is not really happy because he is prone to the same fears and anxieties as any other being. It should be understood that the five aggregates of a deva's existence, Sakka's existence, or a brahmā's existence are all subject to the same fires of aging and death, personality view, and doubt.

Enjoyment of life is fraught with the dangers referred to above, so that at the time of death all the glories of one's existence become meaningless and useless. When the five aggregates fall apart, what one has clung to as one's own life perishes and goes. Whether one is a human being, a deva, or a brahmā, one possesses nothing. Rebirth may be as a lowly being such as a louse, a flea, a dog or a pig, an earthworm or a leech. For instance, on seeing a pig that had been a brahmā in a certain previous existence, the Buddha remarked thus:

> "When the roots of a tree are undamaged, but only the trunk is cut off, the tree flourishes again. Even so, when craving is not totally rooted out with its latent tendencies, this suffering of rebirth, death, etc., arises repeatedly." (Dhp 338)

That pig had been a bhikkhunī during the time of Kakusandha Buddha. When she attained the first jhāna, she was reborn as a brahmā. Then on her death as brahmā she became a human being. When her human existence ended she was reborn as a pig. The significant thing to note is that when she was reborn as a pig, it was only a pig's existence with no special attributes for having been a bhikkhunī or a brahmā in her previous existences.

No pleasure marred with the inherent fire of death is real happiness. In truth it is only suffering. That is why real happiness exists only when aging and death can arise no more. Then, and only then, is happiness real and true. That happiness is called deliverance or "escape" *(nissaraṇa)*—the seventh aspect we discussed above.

The Two Highways

There are two highways. One highway leads to the truth of suffering, the other leads to the truth of happiness.

Consider whether it is knowledge or ignorance that governs the daily activities of most beings. If their activities are undertaken with right view according to the sevenfold proficiency in the seven aspects discussed above, it depends on knowledge. Knowledge consists of acquiring insight into the elements of extension, cohesion, heat, and motion. Ignorance consists in the inherent darkness in one's mind that has kept one from perceiving the true nature of the four elements. It is the dense darkness that has been with all beings throughout the beginningless cycle of saṃsāra. All activities done under the spell of that darkness, whether they are daily chores, the religious practices of a bhikkhu, deeds of merit such as giving, haphazard mental development or learning the scriptures—in short, all undertakings, good or bad— are only acts dominated by ignorance. All actions done with ignorance lead to suffering. They make up the high road to suffering, which has been laid down under the supervision of aging and death since the dawn of time.

Ignorance is not something that needs to be cultivated. This veil of darkness has always been inherent in living beings. Knowledge, on the other hand, is something that has to be cultivated. This is possible only by following the Buddha's teaching. This is an uphill task since it entails eradicating ignorance. Knowledge is the highway where aging and death are completely absent. It is the road taken by the Buddhas, Solitary Buddhas, and all the Arahants who have ever attained enlightenment. It is the road to deliverance.

This is the exposition of the way leading to suffering and the way leading to happiness—the two highways that lead in opposite directions.

Regarding the way of knowledge: contemplating the five aggregates might seem rather heavy-going for meditation practice. Penetrative awareness, direct knowledge, or insight into just the five basic elements, namely the elements of extension, cohesion, heat, motion, and mind, is sufficient.

Pakkusāti, the king of Taxila (now in Pakistan), won enlightenment by understanding those five elements plus the element of the void or space *(ākāsa)*. The Buddha said, "This being, bhikkhus, is just (an embodiment of) the six elements."

Ākāsa means the element of space. The Buddha indicated the cavities such as the mouth, the ears, and the throat to illustrate ākāsa. If one contemplates the five basic elements and the seven aspects to gain insight into the nature of the body, it is quite possible that insight leading to the truth of happiness is within one's reach right now. This is an exposition on the truth of suffering, the way to the truth of suffering, the truth of happiness, and the way to the truth of happiness. This method of exposition, which is the method of dependent origination in forward and reverse order, is most helpful for practice.

According to the method taught by the Buddha in the Dhammacakkappavattana Sutta, the first sermon at the Deer Park, the four truths are shown in this order: the truth of suffering, the truth of the origin of suffering, the truth of the cessation of suffering, and the truth of the path. Suffering is, as we have seen, the real danger and ill in all forms of existence, which are nothing but the five aggregates. The origin of suffering is nothing but craving. The cessation of suffering is real happiness, ultimate bliss or deathlessness. The Noble Eightfold Path is the highway leading to insight knowledge that we have discussed above. The Noble Eightfold Path has been explained in the section on the fourth aspect of the aggregates. Ignorance and craving being co-existent, when one ceases, the other automatically ceases.

For meditation practice, ignorance, as the antitheses of knowledge, is shown as the origin of suffering. This helps in giving one direct knowledge in meditation.

Chapter Ten

An Exhortation Regarding Great Opportunities

1. The Great Opportunity of Human Rebirth

Why is it such a great opportunity to be born as a human being? Is it because as a human being one is free from the lower realms of misery? Is it because human pleasures are really great? No, not at all. If sensual pleasures are regarded as great opportunities, then human pleasures are nothing compared to the celestial pleasures of the heavenly realms. If pleasure were to be the criterion here, the Buddha would have mentioned birth in the heavenly realms as great opportunities. The Buddha did not do so. It should therefore be understood that by "a great opportunity" the Buddha did not mean an opportunity to enjoy pleasure, but one for doing skilful actions or meritorious deeds.

I shall amplify this statement. Merit may be done in two ways: by working for future well-being as a wealthy man or powerful deity, or by cultivating the mind for enlightenment as one of the three classes of Bodhi referred to in Chapter One. The first can be done only in the human world. The second can also be done in the human world. Many aspirants to Buddhahood have, even during the present world cycle, been reborn in the brahmā realms repeatedly. They did not, however, live out brahmā life-spans there, but willed to end their existences as brahmās by what is called "death through resolve" (*adhimutti-maraṇa*) because they were eager to fulfil the perfections in the human realm. When they were reborn as Universal Monarchs too, they renounced the world and practised the perfections.

The point is that human existence is a glorious opportunity for the wise because in one such existence innumerable good deeds can be done that can fructify as good human existences, good deva existences, and good brahmā existences.

I shall explain this point. In the human realm, the supreme glory is that of a Universal Monarch. If a Universal Monarch were to enjoy this glory to his life's end, he would lose all his glory at death and would have no merit to his credit. He would have thus squandered his human existence. If he appreciates this great opportunity of earning merit, he may renounce the world as soon as possible and acquire merit by which he can be assured of many future existences as a Universal Monarch. He can be assured of more glorious existences as a deva, or as Sakka, the Lord of Tāvatiṃsa, or as Mahā Brahmā, or as an Ābhassarā Brahmā with a life-span of eight *mahākappas*, or as a Subhakiṇṇa Brahmā with a life-span of sixty-four *mahākappas*, or as a Vehapphala Brahmā with a life-span of five-hundred *mahākappas*, or even as an Arūpa Brahmā of the "summit of existence" with a life-span of eighty-four thousand *mahākappas*. These are the possibilities open to any wise person born as a human being in one human existence.

If a Universal Monarch cannot renounce his worldly pomp and splendour, he misses that glorious opportunity to earn the above future well-being. So anyone born as a human being should be able to renounce present worldly pleasures for the sake of future worldly pleasures, which may be far greater than the present ones. If one forgoes the opportunity, one would be just like the fool who barters a precious gem worth a kingdom for a meagre meal. Such are the opportunities a person has in the human realm.

As for those really wise individuals who aspire to any of the three classes of enlightenment, they would be even more willing to forsake worldly pleasure. Human birth is the ideal opportunity to gain real happiness. Only one's wisdom and discretion is the limit.

> "That is why the wise man, seeing clearly the benefits in maturing the perfections, and riding the high tide of fortune leading to innumerable glorious future existences, should forsake the meagre pleasures of the present."

2. The Great Opportunity of Meeting the Buddha

Why is it a great opportunity to be alive when a Buddha has arisen, or while a Buddha's teaching is still extant? Is it because it offers one the opportunity of acquiring merit through giving, virtue, and mental development for one's future well-being? Or is it because it provides the plinth on which the edifice of enlightenment is to be built?

Ordinary kammic merits are sought and won in all eras whether a Buddha arises or not. In the dark ages of world cycles when no Buddha arises, there are people of virtue doing meritorious deeds. Therefore, the world abounds with devas and brahmās at those times too. However, the thirty-seven factors of enlightenment are known only when the Buddha's teaching is still extant. That is why encountering a Buddha, or to be living while a Buddha's teaching is still extant, is the greatest of opportunities.

Much has been made of certain virtuous people born with a penchant for knowledge, but such mundane wisdom is superficial. It does not develop into supramundane wisdom. It cannot withstand the onslaught of non-Buddhist or wrong beliefs once the Buddha's teaching has disappeared. The once wise man then reverts to being a great person, content to drift and sink in the ocean of saṃsāra, ever seeking sensual existences like an old ghost wailing for crumbs around a rubbish heap.

> That is why the wise man, seeing clearly the benefits in maturing the perfections, and recognizing the precious opportunity that leads to enlightenment, should exert earnestly after the essential teaching of the Buddha contained in the thirty-seven factors of enlightenment.

3. The Great Opportunity of Becoming a Bhikkhu

There are three types of renunciation for the life of a bhikkhu: renunciation through wisdom *(paññā pabbajjita)*, renunciation through confidence *(saddhā pabbajjita)* and renunciation through fear *(bhayā pabbajjita)*. Of these, the first two require previous accumulations of merit or perfections. The last means taking up the life of a bhikkhu out of expediency: to seek political asylum, to recover from sickness, to take refuge from an enemy, or to avoid the struggles of the worldly life. It will be seen that the teaching of the all-knowing Buddha is the business of the wise. Whether one is a bhikkhu or a layman, the teaching is cherished only among the wise. As the saying goes, "Lions' fat collects only in a gold cup." I shall enlarge on this.

The Buddha's teaching is a great opportunity for devas and brahmās to gain benefit. Hardly one human being among ten million celestial beings would have benefited, not one among ten thousand of them is a bhikkhu, the overwhelming majority are lay people. During the Buddha's lifetime, the city of Sāvatthī boasted millions of Noble Ones. Among them hardly a hundred thousand might have been bhikkhus. "Being a bhikkhu is a great opportunity," is therefore a statement with reference only to renunciation through confidence or wisdom. One who renounces through wisdom exerts for knowledge; one who renounces through confidence exerts for the noble practice; one who renounces through fear exerts for material possessions permissible for a bhikkhu, i.e. the four requisites of alms-food, robes, monastic shelter, and medicine. These characteristics testify to what type of bhikkhu one actually is.

Alternatively, there can be four types of bhikkhu as follows: one who renounces through wisdom *(paññā pabbajjita)* exerts for knowledge, one who renounces through confidence *(saddhā pabbajjita)* exerts for the noble practice, one who renounces through greed *(lobha pabbajjita)* exerts for comfort, one who renounces through delusion *(moha pabbajjita)* exerts for shallow things, lacking self-discipline, due to a superficial regard for the teaching.

4. The Great Opportunity of Having Confidence

There are four classes of confidence: 1) *pasāda saddhā*, 2) *okappana saddhā*, 3) *āgama saddhā*, and 4) *adhigama saddhā*.

1. *Pasāda saddhā* is confidence in the Three Gems because the Buddha, the Dhamma, and the Saṅgha are recognized as being worthy of reverence. It is based upon a superficial high regard for the Three Gems and not on a deep conviction, so it is not stable.

2. *Okappana saddhā* is confidence inspired by the noble attributes of the Buddha, the Dhamma, and the Saṅgha. It comes

out of conviction and it endures for a lifetime, but after one's death it vanishes from one's consciousness.

3. *Āgama saddhā* is the type of confidence acquired by bodhisattas. After receiving recognition and assurance of future Buddhahood, a bodhisatta has unwavering confidence in the Three Gems, which implies an abiding confidence in the merit of good deeds.

4. *Adhigama saddhā* is the confidence nurtured by the Noble One who, having won the fruits of path knowledge, has realized nibbāna.

Of these four classes, even the first is a rare gift. Many who are born in Buddhist countries do not have even this kind of confidence.

One who has the second kind of confidence can revere a bhikkhu whose conduct is far from being correct, knowing the nine attributes of the Ariya Saṅgha to which a bhikkhu belongs.

One endowed with *āgama saddhā* cannot refrain from doing some sort of perfect merit even for a day.

The Noble Ones, who have won attainments in the path knowledges, are endowed with a confidence that is a great attainment *(adhigama)*. They have an abiding confidence in the Three Gems, the upkeep of the five precepts, the performance of the ten kinds of meritorious deeds, and the practice of the thirty-seven factors of enlightenment.

Confidence is a key factor that determines the extent of one's realization of nibbāna. For example, an epileptic has a fit when he hears exciting music. When he is cured of the disease, no music, however exciting, can cause a fit. He remembers how, when he had the affliction, he used to have fits on such occasions, how his heart would throb uncontrollably, how he would lose consciousness. Now that he is completely cured, he feels very glad. On seeing other epileptics suffer the same painful experience at the sound of exciting music too, he would remember his previous affliction and feel very glad in the knowledge that he is now free from it. When he hears of any cases of fits suffered by other epileptics, he feels very glad that he is free of the disease.

In much the same way, the world is filled with occasions for passion to arise, or for hatred, vanity, delusion, pride, etc., to arise.

A Noble One, on coming across such occasions, remembers how in the past, before realizing nibbāna, he or she had let passion or hatred arise, but knows now that no kind of passion, hatred, or vanity can arise.

On seeing or hearing of other people moved by passion, a Noble One remembers his or her former foolishness and rejoices in the knowledge of being free from passion. On seeing another epileptic having a fit, an epileptic is reminded of the disease and is afraid of suffering like that some day too. A wise person is also constantly alert to the possibility of some misfortune on seeing another person suffering due to uncontrolled passion, because he or she knows that passion is not yet eradicated. A Noble One has no such fears, based on the knowledge that passion has been eradicated. Thus, a Noble One is glad when reflecting upon his or her previous defiled state and on the awareness of freedom from passion.

> "O how happy we are in maintaining our lives,
> Unafflicted by defilements amidst those afflicted!
> Amidst people who are afflicted
> We live unafflicted by defilements." (Dhp 198)

On seeing the multitude toiling at their daily chores, in fine weather or foul, full of ego, blinded by ignorance of the true nature of the elements, and merely feeding the fires of aging and death that burn within, a Noble One feels glad to be free from such foolishness or vain endeavours. As for ordinary persons, they emulate the active life around them.

Vain endeavour or "foolishness" *(bālussukka saṅkhāra)* is the sort of eagerness shown by foolish people, who are so blinded by ignorance that they are unable to recognize worthwhile and fruitful endeavours. Vain endeavour is activity caused by ignorance. Again, it is becoming *(kammabhava)* or productive kamma (i.e. producing continued existences) committed because of attachment.

All kinds of futile activity can be seen anywhere, in big cities, at railway terminals, at markets, at seaports, at airports, in busy streets, etc., where the babble of voices makes a constant din. All this hubbub is misdirected, but its futility is seen only by the wise and the Noble Ones—to ignorant people it is seen as a sign of progress.

> "O how happy we are in maintaining our lives,
> Indifferent to sensual pleasures,
> amidst those who strive for them.
> Amidst those striving for sensual pleasures,
> We live without striving for them." (Dhp 199)

On seeing miserable people such as the blind, deaf, dumb, the insane, or wretched beings such as animals; or on pondering over the worse miseries of the lower realms, a wise person will feel worried at the thought that one of these days he or she too might very well share that fate, for he or she has been carrying on the same vain and fruitless activities prompted by the same defilements.

A Noble One, however, while pitying the sufferers, will exult in the knowledge of being free from such a fate. This kind of exultation must have been in the benign smile of Venerable Moggallāna who saw a group of petas on Mount Gijjhakuṭa. This is how a person who has quelled the passions within feels joy at the prospect of the dreary process of psychophysical phenomena soon being extinguished.

This great opportunity of living in the era of the Buddha's teaching is the time for quenching the fires within. This is the opportune moment to extinguish the eleven fires that have been burning since time immemorial. It is the time to leave behind human affairs and cares, and to devote oneself to the eradication of ignorance. Human welfare has been enjoyed often enough throughout saṃsāra; this life is not exceptional. Whether one is a billionaire or an emperor, one's riches and prestige are well worth forsaking in the quest for enlightenment. Even if one is a deva or a brahmā, these exalted existences are useless when the fires of aging and death are still burning within. All forms of worldly pleasures, whether those of kings, devas, or brahmās, are sources of defilements that stimulate the process of rebirth. As such, no pleasure is particularly worthwhile, as all are decaying, crumbling, and perishing incessantly. The only worthwhile task to set oneself is to root out the pernicious wrong view of personality, an illusion that does not actually exist. This task must be taken up at the right time which is *now*. Once the moment is past, the chance is lost!

On seeing such precious time being squandered in the pursuit of the pleasures that this shallow existence has to offer—still craving, still attached, unsatiated, never satisfied with human or celestial glories—a wise person feels remorse, "I too am still craving, still attached." As for the Noble Ones, they exult in the knowledge that they have freed themselves from the craving and attachment that could drag them down to hell. This is the exposition on how the Noble Ones view life, having realized nibbāna within.

5. *The Great Opportunity of Hearing the Dhamma*

Saddhamma means *sāsana* or the Buddha's teaching. The teaching has three main aspects: training for higher virtue, training for higher concentration, and training for higher knowledge or wisdom, as we have seen above. These are referred to in the commentary as learning *(pariyatti)*, practice *(paṭipatti)*, and realization (*paṭivedha*).

> "Since the beginningless round of saṃsāra my two ears have been filled with human voices and human speech, or deva voices and deva speech, or brahmā voices and brahmā speech. All worldly talk only fans the flames of defilements—craving, anger, delusion, personality view, aging and death—burning within me. Never before have I heard this different kind of speech, which is the teaching exhorting me to extinguish these fires and showing me the way to do it. How opportune it is for me! From now on I will use my ears for listening to this most precious and timely sound before it is too late." (p. 146)

Thus should you ponder, Maung Thaw.

End of the Uttamapurisa Dīpanī

1262 B.E. the First Waxing Day of Kason

28th April, 1900 CE

Life Sketch of the Ledi Sayādaw

The author of this manual, the Venerable Ledi Sayādaw of Burma, was one of the outstanding Buddhist scholars and writers of this age. His numerous writings show not only his vast store of learning, of which he had a ready command, but also a deep penetration of the respective subjects derived from his meditative experience. During a long period of his later life he used to spend six months of the year teaching, preaching, and writing, and the other six months meditating.

He was born in 1846 at a village in the Shwebo District of Burma. Early in life he was ordained a novice (*sāmaṇera*) and at the age of twenty he received the higher ordination with the name Bhikkhu Ñāṇa. He received his monastic education under various teachers and later studied Buddhist literature under the Venerable San-kyaung Sayādaw in one of the large monastic colleges at Mandalay. He was a very bright student. His first book, *Pāramī Dīpanī (Manual of the Perfections)* was published fourteen years after his higher ordination while he was still at San-kyaung Monastery. It was based on twenty questions set by his teacher, which he alone among the numerous pupils had been able to answer fully and satisfactorily.

During the reign of King Theebaw he became a Pali lecturer at Mahā Jotikārāma Monastery in Mandalay. One year after the capture of King, in 1887, he moved to a place to the north of Monywa town where he established a monastery under the name of Ledi-tawya Monastery, from which he derived the name Ledi Sayādaw under which he became widely known. In later years, he regularly toured many parts of Burma, teaching and preaching, and establishing Abhidhamma classes and meditation centres. He composed Abhidhamma rhymes (*abhidhamma-saṅkhitta*) and taught them to his Abhidhamma classes. Some of the Ledi meditation centres still exist and are still famous in the country.

He was awarded the title Agga-Mahāpaṇḍita by the Government of India in 1911. Later the University of Rangoon conferred on him the title D. Litt. (*honoris causa*). In later years he lived at

Pyinma where he died in 1923, aged 77.

The Venerable Ledi Sayādaw wrote many essays, letters, poems and manuals, in Burmese and in Pali, and also some sub-commentaries (*ṭīkā*). A list of his writings has been published in the Buddhist quarterly, *Light of the Dhamma* (Vol. VIII, No. 1), together with a biography on which this brief life sketch is based. Most of his expositions are called *dīpanī* ("manuals" or lit. "illuminators"), and became very popular in Burma. Some of these are short treatises; others are larger works, as for instance the *Paramattha Dīpanī, The Manual of Ultimate Truth,* written in 1897, which is a commentary on the *Abhidhammattha Saṅgaha,* a compendium of the Abhidhamma Philosophy.

Several of these manuals have been rendered into English and published or reprinted in the *Light of the Dhamma*: (1) *Vipassanā Dīpanī*—Manual of Insight, *(2) Paṭṭhānuddesa Dīpanī*— Manual of the Philosophy of Relations, *(3) Niyāma Dīpanī*— Manual of Cosmic Order, *(4) Sammā-diṭṭhi Dīpanī*—Manual of Right Understanding, *(5) Catusacca Dīpanī*—Manual of the Four Truths, *(6) Bodhipakkhiya Dīpanī*—Manual of the Requisites of Enlightenment, *(7) Maggaṅga Dīpanī*—Manual of the Constituents of the Noble Path.

The *Light of the Dhamma* has ceased publication, however, the manuals have been reprinted in a single volume under the title *Manuals of Buddhism* published by the aforementioned Council in Rangoon and by the Vipassanā Research Institute in Igatpuri, India.

The BPS has published a few other translations. A revised edition of the *Manual of the Requisites of Enlightenment* has appeared in *The Wheel Series* as Wheel no. 171/174 (now BP 412), likewise, the *Paṭṭhānuddesa Dīpanī* as *The Wheel* 331/333 titled *Buddhist Philosophy of Relations,* the *Maggaṅga Dīpanī* as *The Wheel* No. 245/247 titled *Noble Eightfold Path and its Factors Explained,* the *Uttamapurisa Dīpanī* as BP 420 titled *Manual of the Excellent Man,* and the *Ānāpāna Dīpanī* as *The Wheel* No. 431/432 titled *A Manual of Mindfulness of Breathing.*

Translations of the *Alinkyan* and the *Vijjāmagga Dīpanī* are forthcoming from the BPS in one volume as the *Manual of Light and the Manual of the Path of Higher Knowledge.*

ABOUT PARIYATTI

Pariyatti is dedicated to providing affordable access to authentic teachings of the Buddha about the Dhamma theory (*pariyatti*) and practice (*paṭipatti*) of Vipassana meditation. A 501(c)(3) nonprofit charitable organization since 2002, Pariyatti is sustained by contributions from individuals who appreciate and want to share the incalculable value of the Dhamma teachings. We invite you to visit www.pariyatti.org to learn about our programs, services, and ways to support publishing and other undertakings.

Pariyatti Publishing Imprints

Vipassana Research Publications (focus on Vipassana as taught by S.N. Goenka in the tradition of Sayagyi U Ba Khin)
BPS Pariyatti Editions (selected titles from the Buddhist Publication Society, copublished by Pariyatti in the Americas)
Pariyatti Digital Editions (audio and video titles, including discourses)
Pariyatti Press (classic titles returned to print and inspirational writing by contemporary authors)

Pariyatti enriches the world by

- disseminating the words of the Buddha,
- providing sustenance for the seeker's journey,
- illuminating the meditator's path.